INCARNATIONAL MINISTRY

Incarnational Ministry

Being with the Church

Samuel Wells

WILLIAM B. EERDMANS PUBLISHING COMPANY

GRAND RAPIDS, MICHIGAN

Wm. B. Eerdmans Publishing Co.
2140 Oak Industrial Drive N.E., Grand Rapids, Michigan 49505
www.eerdmans.com

Published 2017
Printed in the United States of America

26 25 24 23 22 21 20 19 18 17   1 2 3 4 5 6 7 8 9 10

ISBN 978-0-8028-7485-6

Library of Congress Cataloging-in-Publication Data

Names: Wells, Samuel, 1965–   author.
    Title: Incarnational ministry : being with the church / Samuel Wells.
Description: Grand Rapids : Eerdmans Publishing Co., 2017. |
    Includes bibliographical references and index.
Identifiers: LCCN 2017012597 | ISBN 9780802874856 (pbk. : alk. paper)
Subjects: LCSH: Christian life. | Presence of God. | Church work. |
    Incarnation. | Church.
Classification: LCC BV4509.5 .W397 2017 | DDC 253—dc23
    LC record available at https://lccn.loc.gov/2017012597

For Mindy

Contents

Preface ix

PROLOGUE: There Is Need of Only One Thing 1

INTRODUCTION: The Ministry of Being With 7

1. Being with God 24

2. Being with Oneself 43

3. Being with the Creation 63

4. Being with God Together 80

5. Being with Child 99

6. Being with the Called 114

7. Being with the Troubled 133

8. Being with the Hurt 146

9. Being with the Afflicted 168

10. Being with the Challenged 185

11. Being with the Dying 201

CONTENTS

EPILOGUE: Precious, Honored, and Loved   214

Index of Names and Subjects   220

Index of Scripture References   232

Preface

Insofar as this is a book about the word "with," it has the same origins as A Nazareth Manifesto. As for its more specific character, as a book about ministry, its origins lie in perhaps four conversations. The first was with John Inge, who invited me in 2008 to address some of his clergy in the Church of England Diocese of Worcester on the power of ministry. I wrote those addresses in the same month that I wrote the original lecture that articulated the practice of being with; and this book marks the bringing-back-together of the two themes.

The second conversation was with Anna Poulson, who was such a helpful dialogue partner while I was writing A Nazareth Manifesto, and who kept saying how much she was looking forward to reading the chapter on ministry—at the same time as I was realizing that I wasn't going to be able to keep it to one chapter. I am grateful to her for her encouragement, and I admire the way she and her husband Mark have embodied so much of what this book is about.

The third conversation was with Joshua Cho and Freeman Huen, who invited me to give the Belote Lectures at Hong Kong Baptist Theological Seminary in 2015. I am grateful to them for an intriguing proposal, an invigorating dialogue with the whole community, and fulsome hospitality. Later the same year, and without any direct connection, the fourth conversation came about, with Archbishop Paul Kwong, to address the clergy of Anglican Province of Hong Kong over the course of eight lectures—again accompanied by kind hospitality and very helpful engagement. Those two visits to Hong Kong pushed me to turn the conversations prompted by John and Anna into sustained thought, which yielded the two-book project that this has become.

Countless other people have taught me and shown me what ministry is about and challenged me to think more deeply or practice more faithfully. My lay and ordained colleagues and partners in ministry at St. Martin-in-the-Fields offer me example, support, and challenge in equal measure. At every stage of my life in ordained ministry I have received similar gifts, and many will recognize their witness and wisdom in these pages. Some people in particular have materially affected the themes and arguments of this book. Thus a conversation with Chad Boulton, OSB, triggered chapter 1, with Rebekah Eklund chapter 2, with Denise Inge chapter 3, with Karl Travis chapter 4, with Abby Kocher chapter 5, with Alan Gyle and Neil Evans chapter 6, with Jo Wells chapter 7, with Charlene Kammerer chapter 8, with David Trelawny-Ross chapter 9, with David Warbrick chapter 10, and with Richard Hays chapter 11. I am blessed to have and to have had such friends, colleagues, and fellow disciples.

When I became Mindy Makant's doctoral supervisor we scarcely knew one another; but as we came to understand and trust one another her courage and dignity frequently humbled me. Being with her through the months and years as she envisaged, researched, and completed her dissertation and brought it to publication was among the most rewarding experiences of ministry I've had; that journey together embodied what this book is about. She did all the real work:

but, in being with, that's the way it goes. She will do much more important work than I. This book is dedicated to her, as a prayer of thanksgiving that presence, attention, mystery, delight, participation, partnership, and enjoyment are the way to glory.

There Is Need of Only One Thing

I want you to think with me for a few moments, if you can bear it, about the nature of anxiety. There are some things in every life, and many things in some lives, that cause us real, genuine, and in some cases constant distress. We may have a job we love and rely on, and we suspect it's going to be snatched away from us; we may have a brother we care about, and we sense he's going to be sent to prison; we may have a close friend, and we fear her increasing forgetfulness suggests early signs of dementia.

What these anxieties have in common is a deep-seated fear that the things we value are in jeopardy and the things we need are likely to run out. It's a profound mistrust that leads us to believe the things that matter can't be relied upon, that there won't finally be enough, and that we'll come to be isolated, bereft, vulnerable, and exposed.

Such apprehension leaves us prone to be manipulated by an advertiser who says, "Shouldn't you get insurance for that, to give you peace of mind?," or by a politician who says,

---

A sermon preached at St. Martin-in-the-Fields, London, England, on July 17, 2016.

I

"What makes you think you can trust those people? They're out to steal your money, take your jobs, devalue your home." But it can also be exploited by a person who wants to become or stay emotionally close to you, who says, "Don't go there, don't risk that, don't explore this—because it might go wrong, could let you down, or be something you regret."

And our anxiety leads us in a number of directions that don't help us, but nonetheless come to characterize our life. One of those is envy. Envy names the way we cease to value what we have and know, and come only to prize what belongs to others. In our anxiety we neglect to cherish what we are and have, and we brood over what lies out of reach and in our imagination constitutes a key that opens the door to where all the candy lies.

Another such wrong direction is greed. Greed is the impulse to fear that we won't have enough and that what we do have is unreliable—a fear that urges us to accumulate what we don't need and can't enjoy, and what will sooner or later undermine or displace what rightly belongs to us. What is Facebook, if not a taking comfort in many virtual friends as insurance lest the much smaller number of real friends proves inadequate in times of plenty or famine?

A third direction in which anxiety draws us is endless deferral, which leads us to maximize our sense of power by surrounding ourselves with options and choices but never actually settling on one, for fear that in the death of the endlessly possible we may experience the demise of our supplies of hope. When we say we are busy, are we really saying that in our greed we have drawn around us too many things, in our pride we have assumed that those things can only be done well by us, in our sloth we have not sat down and identified which are the most important, and in our deferral we have not wanted to let go of any of them, lest one day we might come to regret it? Thus anxiety is the root of most of the deadly sins, transforming what we are and have from a gift to a curse, and distorting our notion of God from a super-abundant source of grace to an untrustworthy curmudgeon of scarcity.

And that's what's going on in the background when Luke tells us, "Now as they went on their way, [Jesus] entered a certain village, where a woman named Martha welcomed him into her home" (Luke 10:38). People sometimes get angry about this story. Most often it's because they see in Mary a stereotype of the passive, submissive female, and in Martha a type of the assertive, dynamic woman, and they're alarmed to find that Jesus praises the one and upbraids the other. But that's to introduce hurt and prejudice that aren't in the story. Gender stereotyping has done great harm in the history of the church and world over the centuries. But this story is more subtle than that.

What's fascinating about the story is that everyone's a transgressor. Martha's a transgressor by inviting a man into her home. At the beginning of the story Jesus and the disciples are going on their way. But Martha doesn't invite the disciples back to her place; only Jesus. Even in our relaxed and permissive times to invite someone of the opposite sex on first acquaintance back to your pad might seem a bit forward. Just imagine how transgressive it would have been in Martha's day. But then Mary becomes a transgressor because, by sitting at Jesus's feet, she takes on the role of disciple, a status considered by everyone then and still some people today as restricted to men. The word "feet" is almost always in the Bible a euphemism for regions not to be talked about. Mary sitting at Jesus's feet at the very least suggests an intense level of proximity and intimacy. Martha's in no doubt that Mary's out of order, but not in crossing gender boundaries: her concern is that Mary's not showing proper hospitality. It's not clear whether Mary lives in Martha's house or not, but

3

either way Martha obviously expects that preparing, serving, and clearing a meal for Jesus ought to be a shared project between the two of them. But then Jesus himself becomes a transgressor, not just by entering a woman's house, but by criticizing his hostess. He's got previous form on this: just three chapters before in Luke's Gospel he goes to Simon the Pharisee's house and a woman bathed his feet with her tears and kissed them and anointed them and dried them with her hair. Simon derided Jesus for letting the woman do it; but Jesus pointed out that Simon hadn't exactly brought out the red carpet himself. Now Jesus dishes out the same treatment to Martha.

Psychologists use the term "triangulation" for what Martha's doing. Either Martha isn't making much headway in changing Mary's mind or she feels the injustice of her situation deserves a wider airing. So she drags Jesus into it. I wonder how many times in the last week you've complained to a third party about a colleague or family member, rolling your eyes and expounding how intolerable it is that you have to put up with such burdensome, unreliable, and exasperating people in your life, when deep down you know that nothing's going to change unless you find a way to speak to your antagonist face-to-face. That tirade is exactly what Martha does. But she goes further. She actually implies that Jesus is ungrateful and insensitive; and, not content to stop there, she orders Jesus about, as if he were a teenage child being dragged into a domestic bust-up. She's so angry with Mary she can't bring herself to use her name. "Do you not care that my sister has left me to do all the work by myself? Tell her then to help me" (Luke 10:40). What started as enjoying Jesus in an act of hospitality has turned into criticizing Jesus, bossing him around, and using him as a casting vote in a sisterly quarrel.

And Jesus is having none of it. He refuses to be dragged in as Martha's cheerleader; and, ignoring Martha's rudeness,

4

he takes her remarks at face value and tells her she's in the wrong. As we've seen, she's so many kinds of wrong. She's made Jesus a pawn in her game, she's overshadowed his visit with the anger of her own sibling dispute, she's told him he's unaware of and unresponsive to injustice, she's implied he has a soft spot for Mary over her, she's ordered him to tell Mary off, she's failed to have the conversation she needs to have with her sister, she's demanded the whole world be more like her. But Jesus doesn't point out any of these wrongs.

Instead, gently repeating Martha's name (in contrast to the way she avoided using her sister's name), he talks about anxiety. Earlier we noticed how in our anxiety we lose sight of the value of what we are and have, and through greed or envy or deferral we scatter our thoughts over many things, thus jeopardizing, diminishing, or even losing what we are and have in our fear that we can't rely on it. For fear of the validity of the one, we obscure it with the false security of the many. Now listen to Jesus's words: "Martha, Martha, you are worried and distracted by *many* things; there is need of only *one* thing" (Luke 10:41-42). Anxiety leads to many; truth leads to one.

There are a lot of things about Mary (at least in Luke's account) that we don't know. We don't know if she lived in Martha's house. We don't know if she'd been part of preparing the meal. We don't know if Martha had any historic reason to be angry with her. We don't know what her Jungian personality type was or where she was on the Enneagram. We know only one thing about her. She sat at Jesus's feet and listened. That was all Jesus really wanted. Martha's bluster, her busyness, her bravado were all a smokescreen, an anxious avoidance: deep down they were saying to Jesus, "Simply sitting at your feet and listening to you aren't enough. There needs to be more than that." That's what Martha really gets wrong. *She thinks Jesus isn't enough.* Mary says nothing, but her actions speak loud and clear. They say, "There's only one thing. And that's Jesus. And that's more than enough."

Why is Mary exalted? Because she imitates the action of God. In Jesus, God's whole attention is focused on us. Jesus isn't fretting and fussing about a thousand things. Jesus is God choosing to be wholly engaged with us. Martha says she's serving Jesus, but her notion of service is entirely on her own terms: she's not giving him what he wants. Mary's service doesn't look like much, but it's a statement of faith. Martha offers food; Mary shares communion.

I wonder what this story's about for you. About what will you say today, "I have been worried and distracted over many things; there's just one thing I'm really being called to"? I wonder who this story's really about for you. To whom will you say today, "I've been fretting and fussing over you in a thousand ways; I realize it's time to sit at your feet and listen to you"?

The Ministry of Being With

I believe "with" is the most important word in the Christian faith. This book describes what this conviction means for discipleship and ministry. In it I attempt to do three things; this introduction traces what those three things are and how the book weaves them together.

The first thing is to explore the notion of being with, already extensively discussed in my two books *Living without Enemies* and *A Nazareth Manifesto*, but about which it turns out I have a few more things to say.[1] In that sense my purpose is further pondering and probing of an emerging theme in theology. The second thing is to set out some convictions about Christian ministry, so this book might stimulate and inspire a person entering, or considering what it might mean to take up, a particular kind or sphere of ministry. Thus this is a book designed to stimulate renewal of reflective practice in ministry, including but not limited to ordained ministry. The third thing is to ponder more deeply what constitutes the ministry

1. Samuel Wells and Marcia A. Owen, *Living without Enemies: Being Present in the Midst of Violence* (Downers Grove, IL: IVP, 2011), and Samuel Wells, *A Nazareth Manifesto: Being with God* (Oxford: Wiley-Blackwell, 2015).

of being with, as distinct from, and perhaps complementary to, more familiar and established portrayals of ministry. Thus I hope to offer some descriptions and distinctions of abiding value in understanding what discipleship and ministry mean. These three respective purposes shape the three parts of this introduction.

Being With

In *Living without Enemies* and *A Nazareth Manifesto* I explore four models of social engagement: working for, working with, being with, and being for.[2] Here I offer a brief summary.

Working for is where I do things and they make your life better. I do them because thereby I'm financially rewarded, I receive public esteem, I enjoy exercising my skills, I delight to alleviate your need or hardship, I seek your good opinion and gratitude; perhaps all of the above. Working for is the established model of social engagement. It takes for granted that the way to address disadvantage or distress is for those with skills, knowledge, energy, and resources to introduce those capacities to enhance the situation of those who are struggling. It assumes that the advantaged have abundance, which defines them, and that they should maximize that surplus through education and training, and exercise it through applying their skills as broadly as appropriate. By contrast, the "needy" are defined by their deficit; if they have capacities, these are seldom noticed or harnessed. Working for identifies problems and focuses down on the ones it has the skills and interest to fix. It then moves on to address further

---

2. I should say at the outset it's not my practice to highlight the words "with" and "for" with italics or quotation marks—this takes a bit of getting used to but before very long becomes straightforward.

such problems, of which the world is never short. It seldom stops to ask why the recipients of such assiduous corrective measures are invariably so ungrateful.

Working with is a different model. Like working for, it gains its energy from problem-solving, identifying targets, overcoming obstacles, and feeding off the bursts of energy that result. But unlike working for, which assumes the concentration of power in the expert and the highly skilled, it locates power in coalitions of interest, initially collectives of the like-minded and similarly socially located, but eventually partnerships across conventional divides of religion and class around common causes. Its stumbling-blocks are not the maladies working for identifies; they are pessimism, apathy, timidity, lack of confidence, and discouragement. By the forming of networks and the creation of a movement, where all stakeholders come together and it's possible for everyone to win, working with establishes momentum and empowers the dispossessed.

Being with begins by largely rejecting the problem-solution axis that dominates both the previous models. Its main concern is the predicament that has no solution, the scenario that can't be fixed. It sees the vast majority of life, and certainly the most significant moments of life, in these terms: love can't be achieved; death can't be fixed; pregnancy and birth aren't a problem needing a solution. When it comes to social engagement, it believes one can seldom solve people's problems—doing so disempowers them and reinforces their low social standing. Instead, one must accompany them while they find their own methods, answers, approaches—and meanwhile celebrate and enjoy the rest of their identity that's not wrapped up in what you (perhaps ignorantly) judge to be their problem. Like working with, being with starts with people's assets, not their deficits. It seeks never to do for them what they can perfectly well, perhaps with encouragement and support, do for themselves. But most importantly being with seeks to model the goal of all relationships: it sees problem-solving as a means to a perpetually deferred end, and instead tries to live that end—enjoying people for their own sake.

Being for lacks the energy and hopefulness of working with and working for, and yet also lacks the crucial with that characterizes being with and working with. It's the philosophy that's more concerned with getting the ideas right, with using the right language, having the right attitudes, ensuring products are sustainably sourced and investments are ethically funded, people are described in positive ways, and accountable public action is firmly distinguished from private consumer choice. Much of which is good; but in its clamor that Something Must Be Done, it invariably becomes apparent that it's for somebody else to do the doing. The alternative to unwise action becomes not engaged presence but cynical withdrawal: multiple causes are advanced, but their untidy details and complexities are often disdained. Full of criticism for working for and working with, apt to highlight the apparent passivity of being with, it lacks a concrete alternative to any of them. And yet in an information-saturated, instant-judgment, observer-shaped internet age, it's the default position of perhaps the majority.

Having characterized these four models and recognized the degree of overlap between them, the next step is to locate them theologically. *Living without Enemies* and *A Nazareth Manifesto* do this by highlighting the shape of Jesus's life, as the Gospels record it. One can see the Old Testament as a study in perceiving the God who is for us—most obviously creating the world and delivering Israel from Egypt—in creative tension with the God who is with us, represented most significantly by the covenant at Sinai and the sense emerging during the Exile that in Babylon God was present to Israel in a more profound way than simply delivering the people from crisis. Over and again Israel protests that there's no use in God being for us—we want to see some evidence, some action; work for us, at least with us.

This is the context into which Jesus emerges: "O that you would tear open the heavens and come down!" (Isa. 64:1). Jesus is presented in the Gospels as the savior, who works for us not by defeating the Romans but by forgiving sins and opening the gates of everlasting life—achievements concentrated in his passion, death, and resurrection but anticipated in earlier healings and miracles. But this is not all Jesus does: he spends perhaps three years, largely in Galilee, calling, forming, and empowering followers, formulating a message for them to share, building alliances, and confronting hostility. One can see the "saving" as working for, focused on a week in Jerusalem; and the "organizing" as working with, spread over those years of public ministry. But that still leaves perhaps thirty years in Nazareth, give or take a spell as a baby in Egypt. And here's the question: If Jesus was all about working for, how come he spent around 90 percent being with (in Nazareth), 9 percent working with (in Galilee)—and only 1 percent working for (in Jerusalem)? Are those percentages significant—and do they provide a template for Christian ministry? Surely Jesus knew what he was doing in the way he spent his time; or do we know better?

This is the theological foundation upon which, in A *Nazareth Manifesto*, having sought to dismantle the stranglehold working for has on the Christian imagination, I elucidate eight dimensions of what being with actually involves. These are my best attempts to describe how the persons of the Trinity are with each other.

- The first is *presence*, which seems obvious until you realize that neither working for nor being for necessarily requires presence: they can often operate from a safe distance. Presence means being in the same physical space as the person with whom you are engaging.

- Next comes *attention*, which turns generality into particularity and transforms "showing up" into focused interaction. Attention requires one to harness concentration, memory, emotion, intellect, gaze, scrutiny, wonder, and alertness here and nowhere else, directly and without mediation.
- Then there is *mystery*. This rests on distinguishing between a problem, which has a generic quality, can be perceived equally well by anybody, can be addressed from the outside, and can be solved using skills acquired elsewhere, and a mystery, which is unique, can't be fixed or broken down into its constituent parts, is not fully apparent to an outsider, but can only be entered, explored, and appreciated. Treating, for example, death as a problem risks wasting energies pursuing solutions, many of which take one away from a person's presence and divert attention elsewhere—thereby missing the call to be with someone as they enter a great mystery.
- Lest all this seem too solemn and earnest, the fourth dimension is *delight*. This is the recognition of abundance where conventional engagement is inclined only to see deficit. Delight rejects the template of how things should be and opens itself to surprise and humor and subversion and playfulness. Delight is glad to take time where conventional engagement is overshadowed by urgency.
- The next two dimensions are in some ways a pair. *Participation* names the way being with is indispensable and unsubstitutable. It diverts attention from what is done to ensuring the right balance of who does it. Of the hundred reasons to bypass being with, efficiency is near the top of the list. Participation says there's no justification

for leaving someone behind, and it queries whether our hurry to get somewhere is rooted in our reluctance truly to engage with the person with whom we are traveling.

- By contrast, *partnership* is more prepared to see how respective gifts can, when appropriately harnessed, together enable a team to reach a common goal. Partnership sees how the gifts of the "needy" person, habitually obscured by the working-for impulse to be helpful on one's own terms, can make unique contributions to common projects. In this sense it comes within the territory of working with, and it indicates how closely working with and being with sometimes resemble one another.
- The dimension that encapsulates and epitomizes all the previous ones is *enjoyment*. This rests on Augustine's distinction between what we use, which runs out and is a means to some further end, and what we enjoy, which is of value for its own sake and is an end in itself. Being with, simply put, is enjoying people whom the world, having no use for, is inclined to discard.
- Finally, *glory* names the purpose of all things: the opening words of John's Gospel ("the Word became flesh ... and we have seen his glory"; 1:14) demonstrate that the epitome of glory, and the originating purpose and final goal of all things, is God being with us in Christ.

Each of these dimensions is rooted in the life of the Trinity and embodied in the life of Jesus, as chapters 8 and 9 of *A Nazareth Manifesto* describe. My concern there and here is not to discredit the other three models but to describe vividly and persuasively what being with actually involves.

Ministry

I understand the Christian life to come in three parts: discipleship, ministry, and mission. These refer to how one's faith shapes the self, the church, and the world, respectively. While my initial reflections on being with, as recorded in *Living without Enemies* and *A Nazareth Manifesto*, largely concerned mission, mission isn't the subject of this book. It's the subject of the book that accompanies and complements this one, entitled *Incarnational Mission: Being with the World*. This book is about discipleship and ministry.

Discipleship is first of all one's relationship with God—a daily walk of grace, wonder, intimacy, sadness at failure, repentance, renewal, forgiveness, longing, gratitude, and companionship. But this can't be expressed in a single, direct encounter. It has at least four other dimensions. There is one's relationship with oneself—one that can't be taken for granted, can be the source of much grief and discomfort, and is not wholly incorporated within one's relationship to God. There is one's relationship with other Christians, understood not so much as ministry but as the need, side by side, to embody Christ together and work out one's salvation with collective fear and trembling. There are the personal relations of life—not those of church (ministry) or world (mission) but household, family, and friends, where one's role is colored, but not defined entirely, by one's faith. And there's the wider universe, the heavens above, the soil, seas, and skies, the animal, plant, and insensate creation, which together shape one's notion of life, beauty, purpose, struggle, and glory. I understand discipleship as being with God as shaped by being with oneself, one's community of faith, one's close relationships, and the wider creation. Thus these are the subjects addressed in the first half of this book.

Discipleship overlaps with ministry in several ways.

Those engaged in ministry never stop being disciples. Meanwhile, there are many occasions when one is "wearing more than one hat" at the same time. For example, when a person gives a healthy percentage of their income to the church, that's an act of discipleship; but when they donate to the fund for putting a new roof on the church building, that's an act of ministry. The first is about their gratitude to God, the second about their desire to strengthen the life of their congregation. It's a subtle distinction. But those exercising ministry need to be able to make such distinctions. For they should be aware of when their own inclinations, preferences, needs, and weaknesses in discipleship come into tension with what is required of them in ministry. For example, it can be hard when one's desire to be a friend—and to keep a friendship—comes into conflict with words that need to be said or choices that need to be made in the exercise of ministry. Again, one's own preferred style of worship or music or catechesis may be somewhat different from what a congregation needs at a particular time; the way one has come to know God or feels most intimate in expressing devotion (discipleship) may not be what's most helpful for the community as a whole (ministry).

Ministry means taking up a specific role in order to help build up the church. That role may be formal or informal. Ordained ministry refers to the setting aside of certain people, usually involving extensive formation, education, and training, to carry out fundamental roles in a Christian community, often including the performance of sacraments, the preaching of the word, the leading of worship, and the convening of the body's decision-making process. Entering ordained ministry means being set apart; and in some traditions this means wearing specific clothes. It's seldom spelled out what these clothes, notably the clerical collar, actually signify. Since the clothes are highly relevant for the ministry of being with, this is a suitable place to do so.

The collar says one thing to parishioner and stranger alike: "This conversation we're about to have, this conversation we're now having, could be the most important one of your life. It doesn't have to be—I can laugh, I can relax, I can have fun, I can just be with you in joy or in sorrow. But it can be. It may not be the right time for you, but it's always the right time for me. I will never tell you I'm too busy, I will never make light of your struggles, I will never tell you something more interesting actually happened to me, I will never say 'I know' when you're exploring a feeling for the first time, I will never change the subject when you bring up something that's hard to hear. I'll never do any of those things because all of them in different ways are saying I'm out of my depth. And what the collar is saying is, I am someone who, however deep you wish to go, will never be out of my depth. You can trust me to listen. You can trust me to withhold my personal investment in the issues for another time and another place. You can trust me to be alert to the ways of God however strange the story you tell. You can trust me to know when some kind of specialized help from another party may be in order. But you can also trust me to know that now could be the time more than any other time for the moment of truth."

One new deacon, a month after his ordination, made one of the biggest mistakes in ministry he ever made. There was a gas explosion and several parishioners were in the general hospital on the other side of town with severe burns. He didn't have a car so he took the bus each afternoon for a couple of weeks to make hospital visits. One afternoon he was getting off the bus and the driver asked him to wait a few moments until everyone else had got off at the last stop. The driver said, "Do you ever hear confessions?" The young deacon was very conscious that he was not yet a priest and couldn't give absolution, so he asked where the bus driver lived and gave him the address of the priest whose parish he lived in. What a fool he was. His clerical collar had done its work. A stranger realized what he did not—that the collar was saying, "I'm not out of my depth in any conversation you are called to have with me." But that afternoon the young deacon failed to live up to his collar. He was so worried about doing the right thing by the procedures of church discipline that he couldn't see that here was a sinner who was asking to meet God, a prodigal who was running to come home to the Father. He gave the driver the address of his parish priest. It's unlikely he ever made that rectory visit. That bus driver wanted the young deacon to help him change his life. He forgot that, in the ministry of being with, the moment of truth could always be right now.

Thus ordained ministry highlights that ministry is to be undertaken reverently, soberly, and after serious thought. But ordination by no means circumscribes the whole of ministry. An act of ministry is any action of a disciple that enables the body to function, flourish, and become more faithful. That can be taken by a couple that volunteers to counsel others who are preparing for marriage; by a child who sings in a choir; or by a person who sweeps the gutters on the roof of the church building. Ministry isn't "helping the clergy" or "getting the jobs done": it's answering the call given at conversion and fulfilling the commission bestowed at baptism to "feed my sheep." The humbler and more mundane aspects of ministry are best seen as acts of preparation and formation for the greater challenges that inevitably arise. Acts of welcome and peace-sharing are good in themselves, but they become more significant when a person returns to a community after a period in prison for a shameful offense, or when a person turns up to worship in a congregation not long after a marriage breakdown in which they were generally supposed to be the destructive perpetrator. Cleaning the parish hall is a worthy task in its own right, but it comes more into focus when the hall has been used to give temporary hospitality to a person fleeing persecution or adverse weather.

One Sunday a preacher felt he'd taken a bit of a risk by speaking explicitly about a war that was under way and that he believed required theological scrutiny. He knew some congregation members would feel uncomfortable. After the service a formidable-looking man, who had a military air and a rosy complexion, asked to have a word. The preacher feared a brow-beating. Instead, the man began to talk hesitantly, humbly, and tentatively about how much it meant to him to receive communion, particularly holding the sacramental bread in his two hands. And he said he wondered how it was possible to become one of the people who distributed communion, since he wanted to be close to the sacrament and bring others close too. He was discerning a call from discipleship to ministry. The preacher was thinking only about himself.

The third dimension of the Christian life is mission. Whereas ministry seeks to know Christ and make Christ known within the body of believers, mission addresses the world—all that has taken the freedom of God's patience not yet to believe. But mission often describes that world as the kingdom—thus anticipating that it will be the theater of God's epiphanies, the sphere of the Spirit's work beyond the church, where disciples are humbled by acts of charity the church could seldom encompass, surprised by goodwill that puts the church to shame, and challenged by examples of integrity, courage, kindness, and wisdom the church badly needs. Again, discipleship often overlaps with mission: when you pause to read and reflect on a verse of scripture while taking a break between tasks in a secular workplace, it's an act of discipleship; when a colleague asks what you're reading, and you perhaps invite them to join you, it quickly becomes mission. Similarly, if you sit on a bench eating lunch, being with yourself and creation, it's discipleship; if you offer a sandwich to a stranger beside you, it's an act of mission. Likewise, ministry and mission frequently overlap or coincide: if you take a group of young people to cultivate an elderly person's garden, it looks like an act of mission (helping the poor); but it may in truth be primarily ministry—strengthening the young people's sense of purpose and helping them bond as a group. Similarly, if a pastor speaks on local radio in a "pause for thought" reflection, they will be speaking to disciples (ministry) and the rest of the region (mission) simultaneously.

It's relatively unusual for people to make these kinds of distinctions between discipleship, ministry, and mission. My two aforementioned books have attracted a degree of interest from those engaged in what's often described as "incarnational ministry." This generally refers to individuals, households, or communities that have made a commitment to live in socially and economically challenged neighborhoods. Many such initiatives share or embrace the kinds of theological insights and proposals I've described in this introduction and have set out in detail in the two books in question. But by the definitions I'm using here, and have just outlined, such initiatives are better described as incarnational mission. While they often have a substantial ministry element (a rule of life for the household, and active participation in a local congregation), their primary focus is on the kingdom—those whose encounters with God have not been noted, named, or translated into participation in a church congregation and have not resulted in active discipleship. I have no desire to criticize such exemplary communities—only to offer such clarifications and descriptions so as to renew their pioneering work.

But I also want to recover the term "incarnational ministry" as not simply or primarily an approach to mission for the few, but as a sustained understanding of ministry for the many. That is what this book seeks to do.

The Ministry of Being With

I've said a word about the first three chapters of the book, which largely consider discipleship. I want to speak now about the second half of the book, which is more explicitly about ministry. The fourth and fifth chapters explore subjects where discipleship and ministry most obviously overlap. Being with God together is about the life of a local church, focused on prayer but involving a host of complementary activities, blending discipleship and ministry. But I've called it being with God together because one of the distinctive features of church is that here Christians regard all their encounters with one another as ways of being with God. The same could be said of the other chapters, but that would be to labor the point. I stress the issue in this chapter because I want to emphasize that ministry is not ancillary to discipleship. It's not that our "personal relationship with God" is everything and the rest is an also-ran. We don't know who God is unless we realize that God has called us to be Christ's body together. That's not something that can be done on one's own. Fellow disciples are not a clumsy obstacle to our own faith; they're the necessary but not sufficient ground of our faith. Baptism is being made part of a body with others, not simply being united with God in Christ.

Being with child is the most provocative theme in the book, partly because its title is subtly different in form from the other chapters, but mostly because I'm a man and, it goes without saying, have never been "with child." Thus I approach the subject with more than usual humility. But I wanted to include it because of all subjects it is the most awesome and the most helpful for illustrating how much of life is beyond anyone's control; and it offers an intriguing way to begin to talk about being with children.

Being with the called is the way I attempt to talk about ministry as it relates to "normal" people. Of course there are no normal people. But I didn't want the contents of the book to imply that being with is simply a strategy to employ with people who are in such desperate circumstances that conventional ministry is largely useless. Instead of the term "normal" I speak of the called, because a great part of being with people in the ordinary warp and weft of life is about their working out their vocation in great things and small, and thus establishing where they belong in God's story. No one is normal—but all are called.

The remaining chapters are perhaps the heart of the book, where I demonstrate one of the deepest convictions of the ministry of being with, that God is most fully disclosed at times of our greatest distress and despair. These chapters don't pretend to be an exhaustive treatment. The troubled are those who have got themselves into a mess, as we all do, more frequently than we care to admit. Next are those who have run into serious anguish, either through injury inflicted by another (the hurt) or through sickness that comes from who knows where (the afflicted); in both cases it's a burden that one may expect to last for a season rather than settle permanently. The challenged are those who seem out of reach because of their profound disability or irreversible illness—those whom society seems to have no use for, who are regarded by many as a burden. The dying need no explanation, but here is the litmus test of being with, because it is the point where working for has done all it can do. When there is nothing to do, being with comes into its own.

Each chapter has more or less the same shape. In every case I discuss the eight dimensions of being with as elaborated in chapter 8 of A *Nazareth Manifesto* and summarized above. I don't always keep the same order, or regard each one in each case as being of equal significance. But the intention is to use these dimensions to come to grips with each context; show just how much vigor they, taken together, offer to even the most troubling circumstances; test the categories and highlight places where some are, in some cases, less helpful or pertinent; and amplify each one so by the end one has a richer notion not just of ministry, and of being with, but of each of the dimensions themselves.

The book is largely a distillation of insights derived from twenty-five years in pastoral ministry: what I'm describing is the person I have wanted to be, the ministry I have sought to embody. I'm the first to recognize that I'm a poor example of much that I propound; but I believe it's nonetheless worth propounding. In many ways it brings together the arguments and reasonings of my three most substantial books, *Improvisation, God's Companions,* and A *Nazareth Manifesto*.[3] The connection with the third is obvious: this book, and its companion *Incarnational Mission,* together form a kind of sequel. Readers of *God's Companions* may feel similarly that this is a second book in the same spirit—one that sees God giving everything we need to follow faithfully, and one that roots theology in the practices of the local church. (They may also recognize why I didn't devote a chapter to friendship here, having written a whole book about friendship there.) Perhaps less obviously, this book also draws significantly on *Improvisation*—most extensively on the ability to overaccept and reincorporate, central to that book and at the heart of the ministry of being with, as this book shows.

---

3. Samuel Wells, *Improvisation: The Drama of Christian Ethics* (Grand Rapids: Brazos; London: SPCK, 2004); and *God's Companions: Reimagining Christian Ethics* (Oxford: Blackwell, 2006).

But this book seeks to be something beyond offering sustained studies of being with, identifying the particular practices of ministry, and drawing together insights from a career as a pastor and theologian. It seeks to be a meditation on the ways of God; a prayer of a reflective, joyful practitioner, grateful for the opportunity to meet God in such privileged settings. Its sentences can be read quickly, so as to grasp some of the dimensions of what being with implies in various contexts I assume the reader has encountered or soon will. But each sentence is also written so that it may be read slowly, reflectively, and over again, as a prism reflecting on faith, ministry, God, and, in several cases, the transfiguration that can come through and beyond setback and suffering. Whether a book can be at the same time a polemic for a different approach to ministry, a guide for its conduct, the advancement and amplification of a promising theological motif, and a meditation inviting devotion and more reflective practice is for the judgment of the reader. It will no doubt be different things to different people. But all of these things dwell in its writing and in the living that preceded and informed it.

CHAPTER 1

Being with God

The ministry of being with begins with being with God in prayer. This is the moment when one's identity as a child of God is simplest and most explicit. It sets the foundations for all other relationships and forms of ministry.

Prayer, like a number of other things, is fundamentally about showing up. Being there is a necessary but not sufficient condition for being with. What this affirms is that prayer is not essentially about words. As in a relationship between spouses, or friends of many years' standing, most of the communication in prayer is nonverbal. When Mary sat at the feet of Jesus in Bethany and took in his every word, we have no record of what she said—if she said anything at all. The point is she sat there, and expected to be filled with glory, and assumed her **presence** was of greater and more appropriate service to Jesus than whatever important tasks delayed her sister Martha in the kitchen. Like Mary, the disciple who seeks to pray must begin by showing up and should take for granted that there's no more important business than this. There may be more interesting, more intriguing, more demanding, or more apparently urgent business—but there's no more important business than this. Thus if one keeps a calendar or diary, time for prayer is the first item to be written in it. All the other urgent things are required if one is to set the world to rights; prayer is a recognition that God has already set the world to rights, and anything that remains amiss only God will fully and finally be able to redeem and heal.

This practice of prayer is the church's answer to consumerism. Every new gadget, every new item of clothing or household decoration or means of transport—each one offers more efficient, more attractive, more multidimensional ways of achieving, completing, or connecting. Each one proposes a form of redemption or a manner of distraction that attempts to bypass the source from which transformation truly comes. Many such forms of technology seek to obviate physical, bodily presence. The practice of prayer thus offers a way to discern which forms of technology build up ministry and discipleship, and which ones diminish or distract from them. If a gadget enhances presence, the likelihood is that it may play a salutary role in deepening ministry and discipleship.

Prayer is the first event of the day. Not necessarily the first thing a person does on awaking, but the first event that makes a day more than merely survival, that points to the source and destiny of all things, that makes a person aware that they are not a self-creator and self-redeemer. The presence of the disciple before God is a recognition that God is present before them at every moment in the power of the Holy Spirit. Therefore presence in prayer is the disciple's acknowledgment in body, mind, and spirit of the Holy Spirit's constant presence.

While this may seem a moment of great isolation—when the busy world is hushed, the fever of life is silent, and the work or pleasure of the day is set aside—in fact it's a rare moment of relief from isolation. The fervid day is a time of isolation, of living according to the understanding that you only get what you acquire and secure for yourself. By contrast, personal prayer is a dismantling of isolation. It is a moment of recognition that you are safe within the embrace of the everlasting arms, that there is one who knows you and your hopes and fears better than you know them yourself, and who watches over you even while you sleep. This is a with that turns isolation into presence. Meanwhile, in such moments, like nowhere else, you're united with those you love but see no longer, those from whom you're separated by distance, difference, or discord, and those whom you have not seen but yet you love—the communion of saints. Personal prayer is never isolated; it's always joining in the prayer of the church, yesterday, today, and forever, across time and space. It is a great moment of celebration, not only that God is with us, but that we are with one another. Just as the Holy Spirit makes Jesus present in the elements of Holy Communion, so does the Spirit make present the whole church when the disciple is present before God's presence in so-called personal prayer.

While personal prayer is a great celebration of God with us, presence also brings a cost. The cost is not just one of time, or physical comfort, or the interruption of a life of perpetual distraction. When the psalmist says, "Where can I flee from your presence?" (Ps. 139:7), it brings a recognition that nothing can be hidden from God. The imbalance between the parties in personal prayer is not just the infinite qualitative difference between creator and creature; it is between the one who knows no sin and the one who knows sin all too well. There are two moments of the confession of sin: one, in the immediate encounter, the unbearable discomfort of being in the presence of God when you have been acting as if there were no God or, at least, as if God were indifferent or unconcerned or irrelevant; two, the "second wind" of confession, when you realize not just that your misadventures have not gone unobserved, but that they have cost God the death of the Son and that they constitute an absurd, self-made barrier to being with God, and that only through God's costly saving action can they and you be redeemed. The practice of presence is the moment in which the first of these two dimensions of confession of sin comes to light. You are naked. However many clothes and barriers and protections you thought you had put on and erected and assembled, none of them has any power. God sees through them all. There is no use in pretending. God sees what you have done; God asks the question of Genesis 3, "Where are you?" and the question of Genesis 4, "Where is your brother?"—and you have no answers that can explain or exonerate. God sees both your sin and the person you were made to be and will one day be transformed into—the person who has been given grace, the ability to live beyond your sin; beyond its division, beyond its damage, and beyond its legacy.

That is the cost of presence: not just the loss of distraction, nor even the dismantling of self-importance, or the interruption of the quest for comfort; more than those, the recognition of what you have been that you were not called to be, and what you have not been that you were made to be; and the realization that there is no truth in you. To be present before God is to recognize the ways in which you are profoundly empty. Which is why few people long to do it.

Attention identifies the moment when showing up✳ turns into being with. It's possible to be present in body, yet absent in mind or spirit. Such absence can be overt, such as the visible distractions of other tangible conversation or entertainment, through persons or materials or gadgets; or it can be subtle, through preoccupation with feelings, events, or pressures that belong "outside the room." If prayer is the first item on the calendar, then the teleological ordering of life entails that one's diet, sleep habits, balance of work, and other commitments should be such that one can give full attention when one prays. If one cannot leave other things alone to pray, then perhaps one is addicted to those things, or overdependent upon them for meaning, identity, or satisfaction. If one cannot think of anything besides one's desires, arguments, regrets, or pressures when being present to God, then one has perhaps allowed such demands, rather than God, the power to shape one's identity.

Attention means resisting the impulse to set the agenda, to control the terms of the encounter, or to asset-strip the relationship to benefit one's own program and skills. It's not selective but takes in the whole of the other; it doesn't begin with a portfolio of types or scenarios, thereupon to diagnose for which the presenting other seems the best fit; it doesn't interrogate so as to catch the other out or find a particular fact or feeling lurking in a hidden place; it has no prior purpose toward which all information received can be applied and implemented; it doesn't jump to a rapid conclusion, forestalling all nuance and ignoring all contrary material.

The relaxed awareness that constitutes attention is neither difficult nor easy. It's not difficult, in the sense that it's not about sweat and effort, about a punishing exercise of withholding personal interest in an earnest effort at empathy, about holding the breath of one's own ideas in order to stand at attention like a soldier on parade. It should be a statement of love rather than duty, of habit rather than sweat, of resuming a shared attitude rather than entering an exhausting interlude. But at the same time it is not easy. Of the many distractions and desires that enter the imagination at such moments, not all are bad—some are very worthy and rightly merit concern and careful thought. The act of faith is to believe that God is looking after them for the moment and to trust that you will not forget that crucial insight when the time of full attention is past. And simply to say that some such thoughts are unworthy is not to say it is easy to maintain concentration and will one thing. But suppressing such sentiments is seldom the answer; what should happen is that attention to God so far surpasses such other thoughts that they are forgotten and insignificant, rather than dismissed or conquered.

One prayer that epitomizes what attention means, and does not mean, in this spirit (and how it relates to enjoyment) goes like this: "God of compassion and mercy, if I love thee for hope of heaven, then deny me heaven; if I love thee for fear of hell, then give me hell; but if I love thee for thyself alone, then give me thyself alone."

Presence and attention are preliminaries for the next four dimensions of being with—in this case being with God in prayer—that follow. A **mystery** is the opposite of a problem. A problem is something that can be solved with the application of skill and experience. A mystery can only be entered, like a great cathedral or a towering ravine or a billowing cloud. God is a mystery and not a problem, and prayer is entering a mystery and not finding solutions to a series of problems.

One aspect of mystery is the other half of the more sober aspect of presence discussed earlier. It's the impossible possibility of sin. Surrounded by such beauty, order, purpose, companionship, and grace, how could any human possibly sin? Why exchange the abundance of grace for the scarcity of fallenness? Why swap the blessing of everlasting inheritance for the pottage of limited satisfaction? This is beyond comprehension. But it still invites contemplation. It's the territory of lament. Lament encompasses not only the absurdity of sin but the disgrace of suffering. Much suffering is of one's own making; some is directly attributable to the perversity, folly, or ignorance of another; but much remains inexplicable, and lament is the practice of prayer that acknowledges the depth and damage of sin, yet looks to God to account for what goes beyond that depth and damage and still weighs down creation, and humankind in particular, in ways that can in no imaginable degree honor the glory of God. Lament comes from a place of deep trust in the faithfulness of God and deep awe at the mystery of creation, which finds itself dismayed at the deep disgrace of events that surely reflect neither God's character nor God's will.

A further kind of mystery is this: How could it be that God could so love the world that Christ should die in such drastic circumstances that reveal both the extent of human estrangement and the inexhaustibility of God's grace? In Charles Wesley's incomparable rendering, " 'Tis mystery all: th'Immortal dies: Who can explore His strange design? In vain the firstborn seraph tries To sound the depths of love divine. 'Tis mercy all! Let earth adore, Let angel minds inquire no more."

The key to the disciple's encounter with the mystery of God is the reading of the Bible. Reading the Bible requires attention, delight, and enjoyment as well as entering into a mystery. The initial experience can be like reading a poem and finding oneself perplexed. When a poem tells a story, the reader can relax. There may not be names, location, or era for the main characters, but one can start to walk in tune with where it's headed. But when the story's obscure or absent, when the lines of verse feel like random brushstrokes on an abstract canvas, when the pressure to "understand" crowds in like an examiner lurking behind the door of a sweaty class-room, it can feel like poetry's an exercise in obfuscation, mystification, and humiliation.

At such times reading a poem is an exercise in attention. It means dwelling on particular words. It involves an attempt to "unself," letting the poem set the agenda, rather than imposing one's own shape upon it. It requires letting the poem teach and lead, on a route never traversed before; it might be taking readers to a particular place—but it might equally be teasing or provoking readers to question why they're in such a hurry to get somewhere.

Finding the patience to hear a poem is very much like being with a friend, colleague, or stranger as they try to make sense of the state their life is in. Sometimes one asks a question, perhaps "So, where does the story begin?" Such an enquiry is designed to give permission to the conversation partner to go a long way back, maybe much further than they'd previously realized, to find a thread that runs all the way through. But sometimes such a question is bewildering, because what the conversation partner is presenting is a series of facts or events that don't constitute a story and don't seem to make any sense at all. What they're speaking out loud is more like a poem. Not the poems of early years education, where all the words are in stanzas and all the lines rhyme and all's well with the world—but a jagged poem that starts and stops and has lowercase letters where you'd expect uppercase ones and where the sentences don't fit with the lines—like a rugged coastline that's been worn down for millennia by the waves but is still rocky and uneven and unpredictable.

The Bible is a poem. It's understandable to want to rush ahead and make it a story, a story that starts with Adam and Eve and goes right through to the new Jerusalem. For it's true, it is a story. But truly attending to the Bible means hearing the ways in which it's a poem, a jaggedy coastline with no tidy coastal path and a lot of bits one has to say over and over and sit with and ponder and allow to abide without making a lot of obvious meaning.

Take, for example, the first chapter of the prophet Hosea. When we read Hosea's prophecy, we know two things—first, that he's passionate about Israel being restored to covenant relationship with God, and second, that around twenty-five years after he died the Northern Kingdom was extinguished by the Assyrians, leaving only the two Southern tribes of Judah to uphold God's covenant ever after. Hosea 1 is a story of a man who makes a reckless marriage, whose wife, as expected, is serially unfaithful to him, and who has three children, forebodingly named Jezreel, Lo-ruhamah, and Lo-ammi. These are obligingly translated as "You'll be without a leader"; "You'll be without God's loving-kindness"; "You'll be without God." The chapter isn't all bad news. It ends on a note of hope. It looks forward to a day when "The number of the people of Israel shall be like the sand of the sea," their name will be changed from "Not My People" to "Children of the Living God," they will regain the land, and the Northern and Southern kingdoms will be united under one king.

But most of that didn't happen. So it yields the question, What's it doing in the Bible if it's not true? That's the significance of the Bible being a poem. If it was simply saying God's in control, humans made mistakes, but God has everything in hand and forgiveness and eternal life will follow, there would be no need or logic behind sixty-six books and three-quarters of a million words. The book of Hosea is not a simple story; it's a mighty challenging poem that leaves us asking penetrating questions—among them, Why does God exercise such savage judgment on a people that were formed and crafted with such love? What do we do with promises God seems to make that God doesn't seem to have kept? What do we do with promises that maybe still can be kept? As with the most tantalizing poems, there aren't simple answers to such questions. Instead, we have to stay tuned, live with the ambiguity, and explore the depth of each question.

But to say it's a poem, and to say it exasperates and challenges and unsettles and sometimes bewilders, is not to say we can simply treat it as armchair theater or abstract speculation. The point is to be with its ambiguity and unresolved tension. As it's inscribed into the fabric of Israel, and as it becomes part of the texture of Christianity, certain patterns of interpretation emerge. One mysterious part is whether Hosea's wayward wife is a real person, and whether God orchestrated the marriage in order to teach Israel a lesson, or whether the whole story is a parable, a larger-than-life extended fable to which God's people repeatedly return for wisdom, insight, and truth. And this is a crucial transition, because it helps the disciple see that the obvious questions, like "Did it happen?" and "Is it true?," are important, but they're not the only questions. Here problem turns to mystery, and frustration turns to delight. "Did Hosea really give this prophecy?" and "Was he really married to a wayward wife at the time?" are interesting questions, but perhaps more rewarding are questions like "Was Hosea realizing that his whole life was like a parable of his people's history?" And "Is the whole story of Israel in the Old Testament a parable of what it means for humanity to stand before the ultimate forces and challenges in existence, and find it has come face-to-face with a personal being whose whole life is shaped to be in reciprocal relationship with us?"

This is how being with the Bible comes to resemble being with and alongside a person as they piece together, from the shattered or scattered elements of their life, some meaning and purpose and coherent thread. What you're doing together is taking what we could call a really impenetrable poem, and staying with it, peering into it, listening to it, until some kind of form emerges, some kind of narrative takes shape. What both parties would invariably like is that the story become smooth and comprehensible and straightforward. But that seldom happens. Joining someone looking into the confusion of their life isn't about fixing a problem— it's about entering a mystery. So what emerges is less like a story and more like a parable. And to discover your life is a parable can be extraordinarily inspiring and invigorating. One pastor sat with a man as he gradually realized that his own narrative precisely mirrored the story of his community: his unemployment matched the decline of the neighborhood; his sadness at not becoming a husband or parent matched the community's difficulty in finding any agency to recognize and partner with its abundant gifts in fruitful ways. From feeling isolated and adrift, he began to see he had a pivotal role to play among his people: his compassion was no ordinary compassion; his transformation could be the beginning of a change in everyone's fortunes.

But ultimately the Bible is more than a poem or even a parable. It's a love song written by human hands captivated, compelled, and coruscated by the Holy Spirit. Yet it's a love song full of yearning, searching, and longing. And the word we have for such a ballad is "prayer." The Bible is one enormous prayer, which gives voice and texture and content and urgency to our own prayers. Hosea chapter 1 is just such a prayer, which starts with our experience of feeling abandoned, naked, forsaken, and alone, giving substance to our worst fears and deepest dread. But it's a prayer we return to, when penitent and conscious of judgment, or when hopeful and looking for restoration. And discovering that the Bible is a prayer is the definitive way in which disciples realize their own lives are jumbled poems, jolting parables, but ultimately fervent prayers. If their lives are full of tragedy, so is the Bible; if drenched in folly, so is the Bible; if spiced with hope, so is the Bible; if incoherent without faith, so is the Bible. Open a random page in the Bible, and you won't know where it's coming from or where it's going. So with our lives—full as they are of so many anomalies and inconsistencies, but at the same time brimming with potential for learning, discovery, and wisdom, the truth that emerges from a parable. The Bible is ultimately a gift to God's people to demonstrate the truth of God's heart. And so are we. The prayer of **delight** is more of a letting-go than a taking-on. It's letting go of the desire to keep the initiative. This step of humility means allowing God to be the creator, and not resenting it. To use a tennis analogy, God always serves the ball: we are always the receiver. To be the receiver allows enormous opportunities for enjoyment and creativity and improvisation; but these can only be experienced once one has let go the need to be the server. Delight means relishing every kind of serve that comes your way. "Rejoice always, pray without ceasing, give thanks in all circumstances," says Saint Paul (1 Thess. 5:16–18).

This is best illustrated by games played among improvisers in the theatre. If actors get in a circle and the first person mimes giving a gift to a neighbor, whereupon that neighbor receives the gift, before giving a different gift to a third person, and so on, the result initially is stalemate and frustration, because everyone wants to know what the gift is and resents not knowing how to use it. But once the receiver realizes the gift can be anything she wants it to be, the game suddenly becomes one of great joy, because the receiver makes the gift into something way beyond what the giver had imagined. This is called overaccepting. It is not simply accepting the gift on its own terms; neither is it blocking the gift as a perceived threat or unwelcome intrusion: it is fitting the gift into a much larger story. That is what it means to give thanks in all circumstances. In another game, an adventurer is showing photographs of a daring journey to a captive audience. The second person is the photograph. The adventurer says, "Here I am jumping off a cliff to escape a bear." The second person mimes the photograph. Then the second player changes position to become the next photograph, while the adventurer describes the new scene: "Here I am grasping a tree half way down the cliff." Again the game is adversarial unless each player overaccepts the gesture made by the previous player—whereupon it becomes hilarious. In a third game, an antagonized and angry person mimes doing increasingly ghastly things to a second person; the second person responds every time with the words "Thank you." Eventually the first person cannot go on: giving thanks in all circumstances dismantles all hostility.

This is the nature of thanksgiving. It's the habit of taking delight in all things—perceiving within them one's dependence on God and one's contingency in relation to a host of circumstances, and rather than resenting that dependence and contingency, coming to relish it. Any story can be told once as a tale of resentment and bitterness, and a second time as a tale of gift and gratitude. To be thankful is to dismantle the power that is held over you, and to work with the energy around you rather than against it. The prayer of thanksgiving is like a dog that ceases to pull against the leash and instead finds endless pleasure in simply being outdoors with a caring master, knowing that the outing will not be over until plenty of exercise has been had.

The prayer of thanksgiving resembles the priest or pastor's great thanksgiving at the altar or table of the Eucharist. Often that prayer is immediately preceded by an offertory prayer to receive the bread and wine and money—and sometimes other gifts—brought forward in a procession. This offertory prayer is a celebration that bread, the stuff of living and feeding, finds its true purpose when it bears the body of Christ. Likewise wine, the taste of the party and the moment of relaxation, finds its telos in bearing the blood of Christ. Money is redeemed and sanctified, but also fulfilled, in building up the ministry and mission of God's people. One could go further and say that the wood of the forest is consummated in manger and cross. This is celebration: it gives thanks for the way every element in creation is being prepared for its true purpose and looks forward to the way Christ fulfills the purpose of every creature. The moment when that true purpose is revealed or disclosed is one of pure delight—the delight described by the person who says, "This is what I was made for."

The difference between **participation** and partnership is that participation celebrates the with for its own sake, whereas partnership emphasizes the different roles of the two parties, in this case the self and God, ways that come to look more like working with than being with. Mystery and delight have described the encounter with the otherness of God. Participation names the closeness of God.

Participation means being in the presence of God, and being united with God. The word that describes this twofold aspect of participation is communion. In the Greek of the New Testament, the word is *koinōnia*, which means fellowship or solidarity. But in the Latin, the word *communio* conveys an even richer range of meaning, because it combines our greatest desires. When we love God, we have an overwhelming desire to become one with God, indeed to become God, to be folded into the wonder of full life and true eternal, abiding existence. That's union. But we still want to be ourselves, our particular, distinct, idiosyncratic, personal beings, in the presence of God. That's being with, or, in Latin, *com*. Union and *com* make communion. Communion means both being in the presence of God and being united with God. God is Trinity, three persons so with one another that they are united with each other, and yet are still three persons. The Trinity is both union and with. When we are in heaven we are so with God that we are united with God, but are yet still distinct persons. This is communion. This is what the prayer of participation means.

The sacraments are the great celebrations of participation. Baptism washes us and drowns us, brings us into the presence of God and grafts us into the body of Christ. It puts us in communion. Eucharist brings us into the presence of God and puts us in union with Christ—or, more exactly, it makes the body of Christ part of us. Communion again. Baptism and Eucharist are both forms of communion, in which we are united with God and yet remain in the presence of God, retaining our own identity.

Thus the prayer of participation means remembering and experiencing the joy of baptism and communion. Communion is what justification and sanctification are striving for. Justification is about us being able to stand in the presence of God, like a child being forgiven by a parent in spite of everything. And sanctification is about us being made holy and being folded into the character of God, like flour being folded into egg and milk and butter. Justification is the com and sanctification is the union. Communion is the everlasting fulfillment of everything justification and sanctification were all about.

This is what it means to say that with is the most important word in the Christian faith.

The prayer of **partnership** is what we usually know as intercession. For Karl Barth, all other elements of prayer, such as thanksgiving, repentance, and worship, are elements of petitionary prayer.[1] This is because, for Barth, prayer is the stating of privation and desire, rooted in humanity's longing for God and for what God alone can give.[2] I have here tried to offer a richer picture of prayer than this. But intercession is still vital to prayer. Intercession teaches disciples what God alone can do and what they alone can do. Intercession done

---

1. Karl Barth, *Church Dogmatics* III/4 (Edinburgh: T&T Clark, 1961), #53.3, 100.
2. Barth, *Church Dogmatics* III/4, #53.3, 100.

in the best way clarifies the disciple's understanding of her ministry and her confidence in God's grace. The two mistakes most often made in intercession are for the disciple not to realize she is with God *alone*, and for the disciple not to realize that the one she is with is God.

The disciple does not realize she is with God *alone* when she appears to address God but instead is speaking to someone else, or justifying herself before someone else, or in some way seeking some credit for her petition. "God, I thank you that I am not like other people: thieves, rogues, adulterers, or even like this tax collector. I fast twice a week; I give a tenth of all my income," said the Pharisee in the temple, within the tax collector's earshot (Luke 18:11-12). There's no need to offer a lecture. God already knows all that the disciple is about to say. The disciple's self-serving spin on events will not sway God's judgment, and a pious sermon that talks about God in the third person rather than addressing God in the second person will prove that the disciple is not really talking to God at all. Intercession is a moment of clarity for the disciple: that clarity is simply this—"All my hope on God is founded." It is a sobering experience of realizing one is utterly powerless to change the past or to control the future. And yet one is in the presence of the one who can make beautiful the debris of what is gone and make perfect the glory of what is to come. This is humbling, but also inspiring and transforming. Being with God alone is a terrifying experience of one's smallness but an overwhelming experience of God's greatness. There is only one thing to do: ask God to put that greatness to work.[3]

The disciple doesn't realize that the one she's with is God when she doesn't make the most of this opportunity. To name

3. For more on intercession, see Samuel Wells, *Crafting Prayers for Public Worship: The Art of Intercession* (Norwich, UK: Canterbury, 2013), and/or Samuel Wells and Abigail Kocher, *Shaping the Prayers of the People: The Art of Intercession* (Grand Rapids: Eerdmans, 2014).

a host of loved and/or needy people, to list an assortment of organizations or institutions, to lift up a newspaper-full of war-torn countries or disaster-laden regions is faithful and valuable and good. But genuinely to intercede is to petition God on these people's, groups', or areas' behalf. It is to put oneself in their shoes, be with them as much as is possible when often speaking from afar, and to plead with God for an outcome they would seek. It may simply be a prayer of incarnation that they know God's presence with them in their time of despair and trial, or that they sense God's attention in the details of their lives. It could be a prayer of resurrection that God do a miracle and transform the catastrophe of their situation into a place of wonder and glory and hope, or that God turn the water of their mundane existence into the wine of the kingdom. Or it could be a prayer of transfiguration that God make their crisis a moment of revelation or visit them in their wilderness and make their struggles part of the Spirit's theater of wonder.

The result of such prayer should be twofold. It should leave the disciple with the great sense of relief at having put the greatest struggles of life where they belong, with the only power that can truly address them. And it should stir the disciple to wonder if she might be part of the way God will answer these searching prayers—if God's being with the person in need might be done in part through her agency, if the miracle is one for her to behold, if the transfiguration is one for her to perceive. Thus does partnership, which begins in the different roles of us and God, blend into participation and enjoyment.

Our chief end is to worship and enjoy God forever.[4] **Enjoyment** is the consummation of the six dimensions of be-

---

4. *Westminster Shorter Catechism*, Q. 1. Available at http://www.west minstershortercatechism.net/.

ing with that precede it. Augustine describes those things we use as that which assists and supports us in our efforts after happiness. By contrast those things we enjoy make us happy. To enjoy a thing is "to rest with satisfaction in it for its own sake."[5] The mistake is to use what should be enjoyed, which we could call taking God's name in vain or blasphemy, or to enjoy what should be used, which is idolatry.

The issue with conventional notions of personal prayer is that they use God rather than enjoy God. The intention is to get the outcome required; God is simply the best means of securing it. Here I have sought to portray a notion of prayer that truly enjoys God. Enjoyment is presence, attention, mystery, delight, participation, and partnership all enfolded together. It's a deeper experience of existence. Besides summarizing everything that has gone before it, the chief additional element provided by enjoyment is that it is the moment when disciples experience God's enjoyment of them.

To enjoy one another is to participate in God's enjoyment of the other: to pray means to participate in God's enjoyment of oneself. God is present to me; attends to me; sees the mystery of me; delights in me; participates with me; is in partnership with me. This is what it means for God to enjoy me. I learn how to be with others from the way God is with me. I discover how God is with me by the way I pray. My enjoyment in life comes not from a good work/life balance or healthy assertiveness training or strong self-esteem or a successful career or a loving family: my enjoyment is constituted by my participation in God's enjoyment of me.

The glory of God is a human being fully alive. The miracle is not just that in Christ God has given us that fully alive human being, utterly in touch with God and utterly in touch

---

5. Augustine, *On Christian Doctrine* 1.3–4, trans. J. F. Shaw (Edinburgh: T&T Clark, 1892), 9.

with humankind. The miracle is also that God, by enjoying us, makes us part of that same glory. Why did God go to such lengths to redeem the world? Because God wanted once again to be able to enjoy us. Why was Jesus's violent death almost inevitable? Because humanity had lost the art of enjoying God and thus could only imagine using (or ill-using) God. Prayer enables the disciple to discover what it means to be enjoyed by God, and thus to enter a realm of being that can enjoy other people and things, rather than simply use them. Thus through prayer do we learn, to use Thomas Traherne's phrase, to "enjoy the world aright." This is the ethic of being with.

God is praise. Glory is an attempt, in one word, to describe being with as a constant state of praise. It is the nature of the Trinity. Concluding a description of personal prayer is a final recognition that in prayer, the disciple enters a realm of being beyond humanity and beyond the world. Saint Paul says, "I know a person in Christ who fourteen years ago was caught up to the third heaven—whether in the body or out of the body I do not know; God knows. And I know that such a person—whether in the body or out of the body I do not know; God knows—was caught up into Paradise and heard things that are not to be told, that no mortal is permitted to repeat" (2 Cor. 12:2-4). This is entering into glory. In John 17 Jesus twice refers to the glory of God that existed before the foundation of the world. This, for the disciple, is both exalting and humbling. It's exalting because, like Paul, the disciple is invited into the wonders of the imagination of God. It's humbling because these are beyond the imagination of any mortal, and remind the disciple of how contingent and creaturely human existence is.

It is in this state, both exalted and humbled, that the disciple may expect to dwell at the conclusion of a time of personal prayer—of being with God.

CHAPTER 2

Being with Oneself

M uch of life is a struggle to be with oneself; and much of the time that struggle is lost. Modernity has in many ways been a quest to establish the self. Where was it before I was born? Where is it when I am asleep? Where will it be after I die? Such questions plague anyone who longs to establish permanent dominion over the territory of the self. For some, the self is an achievement—a goal realized in the fulfillment of potential, in the honing of gifts, skills, talents, experiences—an achievement that constitutes the purpose of life. For others, the self is a discovery—reached through a long journey, of inner exploration, experimentation, or healing—and when that discovery is made one's integrity resides in being true to that self. The great achievement of the Enlightenment was to displace God as the center of all things, and instead to assert the self. What the self's five senses couldn't engage might exist, but couldn't be known about with any certainty, discussed in any detail, or regarded as any watchword of truth.

Yet for postmodernism, the self is a chimera. There is no unitary, objective reality, no absolute, stable truth, no permanent, unitary identity nor any rock-solid, universal foundation. Modernity labored long and hard to replace God with the self, defined characteristically as the artisan of timeless beauty, useful product, or its own existence; postmodernity abandons the self, seeing human beings definitively as consumers, devouring artifacts, all of which are somehow mediated by culture. Such is the context for being with oneself. One contemporary author locates loneliness thus:

> We are marked by loneliness when we register the death of others to us, when we cease to be connected to the things that surround us, and when we notice that we somehow have become something that we no longer recognize as ourselves. Loneliness is akin to the experience of skepticism. Its intellectual affect suggests a gesture toward doubting the very possibility that the world we inhabit actually exists....
>
> Loneliness is not death. Yet we might as well be dead when our only possibility is to be alone, because the worst aspect of loneliness is that it ends the possibility of meaningful experience by translating the inner dialogue of solitude into a monologue of desolation.[1]

Such words cast loneliness not so much as saying "I doubt whether I am able to be with others, or with myself," but more as "I doubt whether it is possible for others, or even myself, to be with me"—either because I realize those relationships are transient and temporary, or because I don't trust that they are fundamentally real at all. The quest therefore is not simply to come to a place of peace about how much one can rely on points of reference and stability outside oneself, but how one can develop such points within the self as well

---

1. Thomas Dumm, *Loneliness as a Way of Life* (Cambridge, MA: Harvard University Press, 2008), 34–35, 40.

as outside. Loneliness is the most explicit way in which we name, given the fragility of all relationships, our inability to be content in being with ourselves.

On the one hand, being with oneself is a bold opportunity to evaluate existence and experience and allow each to cultivate character and clarity; on the other, it's at best a gloomy interlude to contemplate one's shortcomings, failures, and resentments, at worst a confrontation with loneliness and unavoidable mortality. In the words of Jim Cotter, "Miserable are those who, in their insecurity, look anxiously for appreciation from others: they claim everything for themselves, and yet possess nothing, wandering unhappily and belonging nowhere. Blessed are those who have accepted their insecurity, and are content to go unrecognized and unrewarded, claiming nothing for themselves: the freedom of the earth is theirs; never exiled, they are everywhere at home."[2] This is the challenge of being with oneself.

In scriptural terms the language of the self is rendered as soul. The so-called parable of the rich fool in Luke 12:16-21 is conventionally read as counsel about wealth, not least because its setting in the Gospel suggests such an interpretation. But it's perhaps more fully understood as a meditation on self, society, isolation, and loneliness. The parable comes in five scenes.[3]

In scene one, we meet a rich man. No comment of approval or disapproval is made on this man. But we also discover his land produces abundantly. The rich man does nothing to deserve this abundance—it comes from the land, and

2. Jim Cotter, *Prayer at Night: A Book for the Darkness*, 3rd ed. (Exeter, UK: Cairns, 1986), 34.
3. I'm grateful to Kenneth Bailey, whose reading of the parables has greatly shaped my thinking, and whose account of this parable I follow closely at many points. See his *Jesus through Middle Eastern Eyes: Cultural Studies in the Gospels* (Downers Grove, IL: IVP, 2008), 298-308.

not from his hard work; meanwhile, we've already been told he's rich before the story begins, so the bumper harvest is clearly beyond anything he needs.

Now to scene two. Here, in the face of such abundance, we find two kinds of scarcity. The rich man has a conversation with himself. He has a problem. He has nowhere to store his crops. He's overwhelmed. And in this quandary he has no one to have a conversation with, no one whose wisdom he seeks out, no one for whom he feels responsible, no one to whom he regards himself as accountable. He's alone—surrounded by money and food and resources, but starved of people and of love. This is a story not so much about money as about scarcity and abundance, and about which things are good to have a lot of and which are good to have a little of.

Scene three is the pivotal scene. The rich man finds a logistical solution. It's one that deals with the surplus and frees him from the insecurity of depending on the annual crop. He finds a way to cushion himself from contingency, and thereby insulate himself from dependence on other people and dependence on God: bigger barns. He's touchingly happy with his solution. He repeatedly uses the words "me," "my," and "I" in these two scenes. This is about making a world in which you don't need anybody or anything. It sounds to the rich man like a palace. But it turns out to be a prison.

Scene four is a mirror of scene two. It's full of irony. First, the man, basking in abundance, foresees without regret a future in which he has no one to talk to but himself. He sees only abundance and comfort; we see only the loneliness and isolation of a man who has invested in the wrong things. The height of irony is the way he anticipates celebrating his good fortune. He talks about a party: "Eat, drink, and be merry," he says. But he has no one to attend the party but himself. No one to share the banquet, raise a glass, or join the dance. Just him. It's a ghastly parody of heaven, with no God, no companions, and no eternity.

The last scene mirrors the first, turning plenty to isolation. In scene five God calls off the contest. The rich man's bigger barns are useless: useless for making him truly secure in the face of death, and useless, after his death, for offering any benefit to anyone else. It's as if the rich man dies and is buried with the key to his barns in his pocket. In every scene the rich man is on his own: he profits, converses, decides, celebrates, and finally dies—an isolated figure at every stage. He has set out to insulate himself from death but instead he has insulated himself from life—both now and forever. He is—no question—a fool. But his foolishness lies in his self-constructed isolation.

Part of the question here is to engage with a tension that runs through the Old Testament, between independence from contingency and dependence on God. It's an ambivalence between Moses, the wandering pilgrim who depended on God's grace, and Joseph, the prudent bureaucrat who gave security to a whole nation. Israel's search for security is the story of the Old Testament, and the question is always whether Israel will find security in God or seek it elsewhere. The story of the New Testament is the same, except the word "security" turns into the word "salvation." That same tension between the manna and the barn has permeated the church throughout its history—the tension between the naïve Franciscan mendicant and the sprawling Vatican administration.

But reading the Bible as God's story also means realizing that God is a character in this story. God is like a wealthy person, who has everything—more than enough. And yet God doesn't create a fat cushion from contingency, God doesn't invest in insulation, God doesn't devise a scheme to ensure security. God in Christ stands at our mercy; God puts the life of the Trinity in our hands—in the hands of Mary, who carried the baby Jesus with Joseph of Nazareth, and carried the body of the crucified Jesus with Joseph of Arimathaea. And God calls us to invest our security in that same Jesus, with no cushion, no insulation, nothing that the rich man in the parable aspired to, but instead utter vulnerability to God, to the evil intentions and fallible loyalties of human beings, to the contingencies of sin and folly and fragility and fecklessness. Before we're too quick to call the rich man in the story a fool, we might reflect on our resistances to imitating God's way of being rich. If God's security really is us, then surely, by most of our standards, God is a rich fool.

Being with this parable means asking ourselves, "Who are we reading this story *with*?" If we immediately assume we're the rich man in the story we quickly get into a detailed debate about the prudence of saving versus the grace of sharing. But most Christians in the world couldn't dream of being the rich man. Most Christians, from their economic standpoint, are at the mercy of rich people who assume the only question is whether to build bigger barns. The rich man in this story thinks the surplus food is doing more good in barns than in the bellies of the poor. God says he's a fool. The parable isn't saying that wealth is bad or that farming is dubious or even that storage is sinful. The heart of this parable is that the wealth of our lives lies in relationship with God and one another, and the purpose of material possessions and abundant goods is to bind us more tightly to dependence on God and interdependent relations with one another. The rich man is a fool because he thinks he can obtain security by insulating himself from God and other people; it turns out that by so doing he's put himself in solitary confinement now and forever. God's whole life is shaped to be in intimate relation with us; this parable painfully and unsentimentally shows us how much of our lives are invested in trying to make that intimate relation unnecessary. It's centrally a par-

able about the nature, costs, and ultimate unavoidability of
being with.

Just prior to this parable a voice in the crowd says,
"Teacher, tell my brother to divide the family inheritance
with me" (Luke 12:13). A simple demand of working for,
echoing Martha's demand two chapters earlier that Jesus
tell her sister to stop listening to him and start laboring for
her. It sounds like simple justice. But it's based on the false
premise that, if we get the division of material goods right,
all is well and our security is in the bag. Jesus's refusal says,
"Possessions exist to make relationships, not to insulate us
from them." The issue for Israel in the Old Testament wasn't
choosing between Joseph and Moses; and the issue for today's disciple isn't between being secure or vulnerable. The
issue is, how can we ensure that our relation to the material
basics and the pleasurable gifts of life deepens our dependence on God and our interdependence on one another, and
doesn't insulate us from both?

The real questions the parable provokes are these: "Are
you letting the Holy Spirit put your scarcity to work to connect you with your dependence on God and on other people, to unearth their abundance through the discovery of
your need?" And "Are you letting the Holy Spirit put your
abundance to work to enable you to make other people's
neediness an encounter for them and for you with the abundance of God?" In the end, God is both poor and rich, and
God uses both to make relationship with us. What a fool God
is! To seek security in us! Our salvation depends on God's
foolishness. The parable presents two models and invites us
to choose which one to adopt: to be a fool like the rich man,
building a strong room that turns out to be a prison cell; or
to be a fool like God, converting all transitory things that die
into relationships that last forever. Our choice is what kind
of fool to be.

This is the backdrop to an exploration of what it means to be with oneself. We may reflect on three dimensions of being with oneself. First, one's basic *survival*, understood as care for the bare essentials of life, such as shelter, income, clothing, food, and water; one's ability to forge a sustainable existence in reasonable health, comfort, and safety; and one's imagination or faith about what survival might mean beyond death. Second, one's *well-being*, seen as one's ability to embody, experience, and express the abiding goods of life—such as love, creativity, joy, peace, trust, and belonging—in ways that are a blessing to oneself and others. And third, one's *flourishing*, understood as one's perceiving, pursuing, and to a significant extent fulfilling a vocation to a unique trajectory of life in kingdom and/or church that integrates and employs one's personal history—the confused and disturbing elements as well as the proud and satisfying parts—a process perhaps best expressed in the words, "Strive to be what only you can be; strive to want what everyone else can have as well."[4]

This is not the same as a hierarchy of needs. In significant ways it's the opposite. A hierarchy of needs such as that of Abraham Maslow argues that one cannot function if one's physical needs aren't met, and one's ability to thrive in the layers above—safety, love, esteem, and actualization—is inhibited if needs in the level below aren't realized.[5] Consider by contrast Jesus's words, "If any want to become my followers, let them deny themselves and take up their cross and follow me. For those who want to save their life will lose it, and those who lose their life for my sake, and for the sake of the gospel, will save it. For what will it profit them to gain the whole world and forfeit their life?" (Mark 8:34-36). He's

---

4. I learned these words from Tom Cullinan, OSB, who attributes them to Lanza del Vasto.

5. See http://www.simplypsychology.org/maslow.html.

saying that fulfilling one's vocation will jeopardize one's survival and quite possibly jettison one's well-being. But this is the crucial point. Following such a vocation is often portrayed as a neglect of self-care (as the phrase "deny yourself" implies). Yet in reality, as Jesus goes on to make clear, it's simply self-care on a longer timescale: "those who lose their life for my sake, and for the sake of the gospel, will save it." Thus the three aspects of being with oneself aren't a hierarchy, or a pyramid—in the light of eternity, they're a circle: the third and the first meet around the back.

The strain of being **present** to oneself is about withstanding the impulse to divert life into perpetual distraction. This may be because life is too distressing, dull, or deathly.

The challenge when life is *distressing* is to resist the temptation to close one's eyes (or escape to wonderland) until the crisis goes away. For some, the fervid intensity of danger, of anxiety, of unknown outcome can make life more tangible, more meaningful, more involved than ever before: the adrenaline is running, the emotional barometer is lively, the heartbeat is thudding. Many look back on such episodes as times when they were more deeply aware of what they wanted, needed, loved, craved; moments when senses were sharp and insight was clear. But perhaps more common is the experience that pain, sorrow, anger, injury, regret, disappointment, fear, hurt, loneliness, humiliation, or failure is so deep that it's more or less unendurable—and escape into distraction seems the only way to buy time for a while or forever.

It may be that being with oneself at such times truly is unendurable, and that it can only be sustained, for a period, by being with God and being with others. The psalms are full of such moments. "Out of the depths I cry to you, O Lord. Lord, hear my voice!" says Psalm 130: "Let your ears be attentive to the voice of my supplications!" (verses 1–2). In a more popular vein, the Harry Nilsson song "I can't live if living is without you" was written in the late 1960s by Pete Ham and Tom Evans, both of whom later committed suicide. But the inability to be with oneself may be somewhat different to the suffering of heartbreak, discomfort, or isolation. It may be more about self-rejection. However much one is loved by others, it may seem an insuperable challenge to love oneself. Distraction may seem infinitely preferable to lapsing into self-loathing.

Self-loathing can be a fury at one's own limitations—failures, weaknesses, shortcomings of appearance, intelligence, flair, social graces, courage; or it can be mortification for one's sins, betrayals, cruelties, selfishness, envy, meanness. The counsel to "love oneself" can be profoundly unhelpful if it's heard as advice to accept sin or repent of limitation. To be with oneself means to find ways to separate sin from limitation and to embark on a process of forgiving and being reconciled with the former while accepting and coming to terms with the latter. What's vital is to avoid accepting what must be repented of or repenting of what must be accepted. Confusing the two constitutes much of the discomfort of being with oneself. By contrast, loving oneself requires a willingness to repent of sin and accept limitation—widely recognized as "the serenity to accept the things I cannot change and the courage to change the things I can."[6]

The flipside of life seeming too challenging is life becoming dull. If one's need for survival or desire for well-being have not been met, then one's life is distressing; if they have been met but one's flourishing is elusive, then life may well be dull. If one is missing the drama of a crisis it becomes tempting to make a drama out of the trivial, just for the thrill of the

---

6. Reinhold Niebuhr, *The Essential Reinhold Niebuhr: Selected Essays and Addresses*, ed. Robert McAfee Brown (New Haven: Yale University Press, 1987), 251.

quickened heartbeat; and a drama often requires an audience, so out of boredom comes not just a crisis but a host of third parties drawn in to gasp or shriek or yell. Such can be the seduction of social media—the impulse to seek in the reactions of others a weathervane for or an amplification of one's own underwhelming reality, the desire for perpetual "news" to substitute for the novel in the absence of the substantial, and the urge to inflate the ordinary in an effort to stimulate the listless.

Thus the challenges of being with oneself in the face of the distressing and the dull can become avenues into addiction. For a drug is the archetypal form of distraction, one that takes away the acuteness of pain and/or amplifies the luster of the flaccid. And addiction is the best analogy for sin: for sin is fundamentally distraction from the reality of being with oneself, with God, with one another, and with the creation.

But there is also the challenge of the *deathly*. Being present to oneself is hard because of the inevitability of death. What makes one mortgage the present tense in an effort to preserve it in photograph or indelible memory? Is it not a desperate and yet doomed desire to shore up one's existence against mortality? The deeper human task is to try not to record, retain, or embellish one's life; but to live it.

How then, in the face of this undertow of distraction, much of which is a symptom of despair, can one be with oneself? This is the territory of **attention, mystery**, and **delight**. The eighteenth-century priest Jean de Caussade, spiritual director to a convent of French nuns, wrote a book called *The Sacrament of the Present Moment.*[7] In it he coached the nuns in the most difficult spiritual practice of all: staying in the present tense. We can't meet God by relying on past stories

7. Jean de Caussade, *The Sacrament of the Present Moment* (New York: HarperCollins, 1989).

or future hopes. We must be present in this very moment now—not just to God, but to one another. For John Calvin, beginning to be with oneself means paying attention. "Nearly all the wisdom we possess, that is to say, true and sound wisdom, consists of two parts: the knowledge of God and of ourselves."[8] Paying attention to oneself means finding joy in the attainment and sustenance of wellbeing: it means learning one's own rhythms and patterns and developing good habits and tastes. It means coming to understand, appreciate, and discern one's body, mind, and spirit and finding the blend of exercise, adventure, diet, and relaxation that constitutes health. The great twelfth-century physician and mystic, Hildegard of Bingen, in her book *Causae et Curae*, describes her practice.[9] She would observe her patients' color, animation, eyes, and vitality; their forehead, hands, and feet; their rate and comfort of breathing; their enthusiasm, reluctance, energy; their temperament, be it melancholic, sanguine, choleric, or phlegmatic; finally, their blood and urine. Then she would gauge the patients' "regime." A regime was a rule of life, covering food, sleep, exercise, even sexual activity. It varied according to age, the season of the year, and the climate of their dwelling place. The principle of a regime is expressed by the phrase, "Even without a doctor you have three doctors at hand: Dr. Diet, Dr. Quiet, and Dr. Merryman." Dr. Diet prescribed food and drink, what and how much to take, and what to avoid; Dr. Quiet, measures and styles of exercise, sleep, and rest; Dr. Merryman, how much sex to have and what kind of emotion to seek.[10]

8. John Calvin, *Institutes of the Christian Religion*, 1.1, ed. John T. McNeill, trans. Ford Lewis Battles (Philadelphia: Westminster, 1960), 1:35.

9. My reading of Hildegard is indebted to Victoria Sweet, *God's Hotel: A Doctor, a Hospital, and a Pilgrimage to the Heart of Medicine* (New York: Riverhead, 2012).

10. Sweet, *God's Hotel*, 142–44.

This is the kind of attention that enables being with oneself. It means becoming one's own friend, to some extent one's own physician, and certainly one's own coach. When Aristotle describes virtue as the mean between two extremes, he is outlining something akin to Hildegard's notion of a healthy regime.[11] This is not about obsession with details. Clearly well-being is not everything; clearly also, it is possible to fall not into distraction, but into its opposite, obsession. This is not about worshiping the self. It is about getting one's body, mind, and spirit into a rhythm by which well-being is a daily habit, not a frequent and draining lurch from hiatus to hiatus, feast to famine, boom to bust.

Mystery is being aware that one is not isolated: one has a story and that story is indebted to and inseparable from other stories. Here is an exposition of mystery ordered as training in being with oneself.

Be humble. Remember what it took for you to be here; to think of the imagination of God that brought creation into being—for there could instead have been nothing. Dwell on the many layers of evolution or whatever it took to get from a twinkle in God's eye to the living breathing being that you are. Reflect on how many of your ancestors clung to life to the point where they could conceive the one whose birth eventually led to yours. Realize by how fragile a thread their existence hung, and how the miracle of your birth is made up of a constellation of other such miracles. And as you contemplate your parents, as you come to terms with both their ordinariness and their fallibility, accept that you would not be here at all without them.

Be grateful. Lord Mountbatten said of Gandhi, "You

11. Aristotle, *The Nicomachean Ethics*, 2.8 (Oxford: Oxford University Press, 1990), 43–45.

would never guess how many people it takes and how much it costs to keep that man in poverty." But it requires a myriad of angels to keep any single one of us in the life to which we are accustomed. We take for granted that others toil in fields and work in slaughterhouses and travel the earth to bring food to our grocery stores; all we do is produce a card and pay for it. We assume someone will labor night and day to make roads and vehicles and bring oil out of the ground so we can move around. We seldom ask whose sweat produced our shoes, our computer, our shirt (which we boast of having bought so cheaply), and we scarcely pause to consider, when we get a bargain, which link in the supply chain got no reward this time.

Be your own size. There are 300 billion stars in our own galaxy and a hundred billion galaxies in the universe. Before you tell everyone not to start the party until you arrive, take in the enormity of that reality of which you are the very tiniest ingredient. Before you say to someone, "Do you know who I am?" ask yourself, in light of the scale of the universe, and its venerable age, "Who exactly am I?" Look at the earth, which you share with so many living beings. Many of the tiny ones scurry and multiply and in hidden ways make it possible for you to breathe, to heal, to digest, to sleep. Realize how you take for granted, when the sun sets, that it will rise again next day. If it wasn't so, what could you do about it? Your life rests in an ecology you will never live long enough to comprehend, still less thank.

Be gentle. Remember the physician's mantra, "First, do no harm." In the words of William Blake, "We are put on earth a little space, That we may learn to bear the beams of love." There's so much that we've never even paused to imagine. When we look to right and left, we see others who know more or less as little as we do. People tend to do the best they can with what they have and what they know. A little compassion, a little generosity of heart, inclines us to look to our fellow creatures with gentleness rather than bitterness, anger, or condemnation. How often have you looked upon what another person said or did with horror, fury, or scorn, only to find yourself, ten years (or ten minutes) later, saying or doing much the same as them? Be sparing with your horror, fury, and scorn, lest they rebound on you and make you lamentable in your own sight.

Be a person of praise and blessing. Recognize that had God not called Abraham there would be no covenant; had God not brought the Hebrews through the Red Sea there would only have been slavery; had God not restored Israel there would have been perpetual exile. Remember that had God not dwelt with us in Christ we would not know we were children of a heavenly Father, made to be God's companions, empowered with the Holy Spirit. If Christ had not died in agony we would not have discovered we mean everything to God. If Christ were not risen we would not know our future is in God forever. If the Spirit had not come we would not know the joy of this good news today. If we had not the gift of baptism we could not enjoy all these wonders through the church. Like Israel, we were made to be companions to God and a blessing to the creation. No more, and no less.

And when you have taken these steps of humility—the awareness of God, of our neighbor, of the universe, of the weak, and of the church—turn over the coin of humility and see that you have been washed in the Jordan, anointed by the Spirit, crowned as one of God's kingdom of priests, and clothed with power from on high. Wash one another's feet, be the servant and slave of all, make every act of your life a sacrament of love to others and praise to God: for your existence is a miracle, and your redemption is amazing grace. And never cease from singing.[12]

Delight is the finding of hidden and surprising treasures amid the green field of oneself. Sometimes those arise from unearthing previously unknown or unaffirmed talents; more often, it comes from the conversion of aptitudes into skills through education and training, application and regular habit. Delight is about joining a late starters' orchestra, about taking up rock and roll dance classes, about developing green fingers in a newly acquired garden, about discovering still-life painting, about learning cross-stitch or starting to cycle long distances. It's about taking pleasure in being with oneself not because the activity makes one fit, or wins acclaim, or produces food, or attracts a partner, but because through it one discovers one's limbs, one's fingers, one's eye, and develops one's touch, one's taste, one's smell. Delight takes the two-dimensional and makes it three-dimensional, adding texture, depth, quality to what had previously been passing, superficial, or ordinary. It turns still waters into a fountain of life.

Participation and **partnership** expand the notion, already noted in speaking about attention, of becoming one's own friend. Participation is the essence of with—in this case, the sheer rejoicing in being alive, the consciousness of breathing, eating, awaking, moving, speaking, the ability both to live and to be aware that one lives, the naming, cherishing, relishing, and celebrating of embodied, mindful, enspirited existence. Most of life isn't experienced like that—but more as a relentless struggle for advantage, pondering of regret, planning for new possibility, enduring of hardship, desire for

12. Slightly adapted from Samuel Wells, "Faith Matters: Desired Things," *Christian Century* 132, no. 11 (May 27, 2015): 35.

elusive fulfillment. Participating with oneself means being able to detach past frustration and future fear and simply dwell in the present tense.

Those who live with a severe inherited or acquired physical disability or impairment have much to teach about this sense of participation. When people facing such challenges receive wide public attention it invariably highlights particular individuals' ability to overcome their physical limitations and achieve great things: it becomes a tale of the triumph of the human will and spirit. But perhaps more important, and more common, is what it means to accept one's physical limitations, even or especially when they are much more considerable than most people's, and learn to love and enjoy the body you have, rather than covet the body someone else has. "We're all disabled—in some people you can't see it" is a helpful slogan; but it carries more authority coming from a person in whom you can see it, but who nonetheless has found ways to be with himself or herself that inspire imitation and provoke emulation. When people become exasperated as they advance into old age, this same ability to be with oneself is often the point at issue. It takes patience, forbearance, gentleness, and persistence—qualities valuable at every stage of life, but indispensable in old age.

A related place of learning and understanding concerns those whose disability is intellectual and whose apprehension of the world can sometimes exhibit an engaging naïveté and attractive simplicity. Such people can offer an example to those who find it hard to be with themselves. It's not uncommon for people to speak of being transformed by being with a child with profound intellectual and/or physical disability. It may be that such transformation is attributable to the infectious way such persons can take their own existence for granted, and evidently be free of the protracted self-doubt, self-criticism, and anxiety that pervades so many adult lives.

59

Perhaps this is near the secret of Jesus's mysterious words, "Unless you change and become like children, you will never enter the kingdom of heaven. Whoever becomes humble like this child is the greatest in the kingdom of heaven" (Matt. 18:3–4).

Partnership refers to working to best effect by apportioning the tasks to the most suitable people. Partnership with oneself means being aware of one's location across time and among others. Being with oneself across time means recognizing that one may be young, and expect one day to be old; or one may be old, having once been young. "For everything there is a season, and a time for every matter under heaven: ... a time to weep, and a time to laugh; a time to mourn, and a time to dance; ... a time to embrace, and a time to refrain from embracing; ... a time to keep, and a time to throw away; ... a time to keep silence, and a time to speak" (Eccles. 3:1–7). To say "I can't do this" may be a cause of anger, disappointment, or impatience; but such feelings may be transformed by the ability to say "I can do this—but this is not the season." Being with oneself among others means wanting to say "I would like to have done this," or "I feel I should do this," and instead being able to say "I'm perhaps not the right person to do this," or "It's clear another person would be more suitable to do this than me." Thus is being with oneself turned from the self-absorbed cultivation of envy, resentment, and avarice into a harmonious understanding of the flourishing of oneself alongside the flourishing of others.

The calling to be with is an invitation to **enjoy** others rather than to use them. That requires one to enjoy, rather than use, oneself. When the satirist Oscar Wilde was asked by his hostess at a party, "Mr. Wilde, are you enjoying yourself?" and replied, "Madam, there is nothing else here to enjoy," he was assuming people were to be used rather than truly enjoyed; but his riposte points to something important about enjoying oneself. When John Wesley instructed his followers to consider themselves the first among the poor they were called to serve, he was helpfully breaking down the false distinction about attending to the self and being with others.[13] But he was also correct in pointing to the fact that enjoying oneself is not, unlike enjoyment in general, an end in itself. It is a precursor to the enjoyment of others and of God. The point here is that it's an indispensable precursor.

Mindfulness is a much-practiced and widely discussed way of attending to present emotions, thoughts, and sensations, enhanced by meditation, rooted in Buddhist traditions.[14] In its emphasis on presence and attention it has clear resemblances to aspects of being with oneself: some advocates use alternative terms such as attention, inspection, recollection, retention, or presence. It is valued as a way to deal with emotions, to reduce stress, anxiety, and depression, and to treat drug addiction, in schools, prisons, and in hospitals, particularly among those suffering post-traumatic conditions. The question with mindfulness is not whether it grasps the significance of presence and attention; it's whether it is truly about enjoying, rather than using, or at least working with oneself. There is so much emphasis in mindfulness on its applicability to various pathologies and its usefulness toward assorted goals; the issue then is whether it is indeed an end in itself, or a really effective and holistic means to an end. Being with oneself is ultimately sharing, for a moment or more, in God's enjoyment of oneself. It's not clear that this is the case for mindfulness.

Finally, to **glory**. It's common for theologians to quote

13. John Wesley, *The Sermons of John Wesley*—Sermon 89, "The More Excellent Way," at http://wesley.nnu.edu/john-wesley/the-sermons-of -john-wesley-1872-edition/sermon-89-the-more-excellent-way/.

14. Mark Williams and Danny Penman, *Mindfulness: A Practical Guide to Finding Peace in a Frantic World* (London: Little, Brown, 2011).

the words of Irenaeus, "The glory of God is a human being fully alive."[15] The sentence has two meanings. One refers to Jesus—Jesus is fully alive, Jesus is fully God, and the glory of God is the meeting of full divinity and full humanity in the life of Jesus. The other meaning refers to humanity. The most apt form of worship is the full implementation of the gifts and opportunities of the person, the thorough engagement with the wonders and mysteries of creation, and the unabashed embodiment of the grace and mercy of the gospel. Such is glory. God wants, asks, or expects nothing more. That is the aspiration of being with oneself.

15. Irenaeus of Lyons, *Adversus haereses* (*Against Heresies*), 4.34.5–7. See http://www.earlychurchtexts.com/public/irenaeus_glory_of_god_ humanity_alive.htm.

CHAPTER 3

Being with the Creation

I consider being with the creation as discipleship rather than mission because I understand being with creation as fundamentally about worship. Not worship of the creation itself—but worship of the creator through the icon, the sacrament, the wonder of creation. To speak of seeking the creation's conversion is absurd—it points up the difference between an animal, that can trust, and a person, who can believe. Mission isn't the right way to think about changing humankind's relationship with the planet's ecology—for mission, in this sense, is less about changing the earth than it is about changing the hearts and minds of the people who dwell upon it. Humankind has, in many respects, lost the art of relating to the world in godly ways—of being with creation; but this is a question of discipleship and holiness rather than of mission.

It begins, needless to say, with **presence**. When David takes on Goliath he has only five smooth stones. But he's spent most of his life outdoors. He's developed the patience of the shepherd boy and learned the rhythms of sun, moon, and stars; he's sharpened his wits by learning about slings, stones, sheep—and picked up tricks from eagles, wildcats, and falcons; he's learned about his own capacities and limitations, such that he realizes Saul's armor will be no use to him; and he's learned about how God is close to him when he cherishes, applies, and remains humble before the wisdom of the created world. The Bible relishes the different settings of wilderness and desert, village and pasture, town and city, lake, river, and sea: it's not that one context is blessed and the others of lesser worth; the point is how we couldn't have the whole story of the Bible without all of these settings. A life that's spent largely indoors and is restricted to the city—and an existence that's immersed in electronic gadgets and rapid forms of transport—is one that is always in danger of losing touch with the hours, the seasons, the source of food, and the perils of subsistence. The eyes that never behold the stars lack a nightly reminder of the smallness of the earth in the universe.

One area where **attention** is especially significant for being with the creation is in the appreciation of the complexity and flawed nature of the world. The church is in the world, and in great part the church shares this flawed character; sometimes it exceeds it, whether by the degree of its crimes, or because the gifts it has been given make its failures the more culpable. "Lilies that fester," as Shakespeare says, "smell far worse than weeds" (Sonnet 94). To attend to the creation is to recognize both its interdependence and its brutal ruthlessness; both its dazzling beauty and its raw competition for resources; both its endless fecundity and its constant consumption of life. Close attention to anything should dismantle sentimentality: constant attention to the creation should make the disciple and the church grateful for the relative comfort and security of their surroundings and mindful of the precarious existence of most creatures on earth.

As the fourteenth-century warrior-king of Scotland Robert Bruce, hiding on Rathlin Island, legendarily watched a spider try and try again to connect its web across the roof of a cave, thereby inspiring him to continue his battles against the English, so paying attention to creation offers countless lessons in patience and perseverance, courage and selflessness. The congregation that heartily sings the words, "Summer and winter, and springtime and harvest, Sun, moon and stars in their courses above, Join with all nature in manifold witness To Thy great faithfulness, mercy and love," as many congregations do, may be moved to match detailed attention to its ardent proclamation.[1] Attention shows that creation is not simply beautiful, or simply dangerous, but full of surprises and distresses and unknowns. In the face of grief and loss, a congregation may well take a traverse through the animal or plant kingdom to place the human life cycle in a wider, and humbling, context. A prayer of lament and dismay can quickly turn to a prayer of thankfulness and praise.

What attention requires is to see God as the giver of superabundant channels of grace. "The world," as Gerard Manley Hopkins puts it, "is charged with the grandeur of God. It will flame out, like shining from shook foil." This is an inexhaustible gift: "nature is never spent; There lives the dearest freshness deep down things."[2] Attention means perceiving that dearest freshness and shaking that shining foil. To pray outdoors, particularly in the fresh air of relative solitude, is to behold a heavenly host of items that can be seen as windows into God's mercy. In George Herbert's words,

A man that looks on glass,
On it may stay his eye;

1. Thomas Chisholm, "Great Is Thy Faithfulness," at https://www.hymnary.org/text/great_is_thy_faithfulness_o_god_my_fathe.
2. Gerard Manley Hopkins, "God's Grandeur," at http://www.poetryfoundation.org/poem/173660.

Or if he pleaseth, through it pass,
And then the heav'n espy.[3]

To pay attention to God amid the creation is to pass through its glass and espy heaven. The extent, delicacy, depth, quality, interdependence, detail, longevity, and ingenuity of the creation evoke a depth of **mystery**. There may not be an apologetically valid argument from design, but there most certainly is a devotionally persuasive testimony of God's dynamic vision. The abundance of the creation is itself a sign of grace: there simply is far more than is necessary for bringing about any ordered purpose: therefore its glory lies beyond any ordered purpose, and in significant part creation's superfluity is for its own sake. What mystery is this.

Yet despite its apparent order, its astonishing interconnectedness, its limitless logic and unfolding variety, the creation is remarkably ordered for God to be with us. It is a theatre of being with. God had no being without the design to be with us. There is no being in God that is not shaped to be with us in Christ. There is no Christ without the eternal Trinity, and there is no eternal Trinity without the Christ who is shaped to be with us as a fully human companion. There is far more creation than is needed for God to be with us, but being with us is the reason for the creation, as far as we can tell, and as far as, in the scripture, we have been told.

The sheer wonder of the created world yields limitless **delight**. In two famous poems William Wordsworth captures the way the created world moves the soul. Wandering "lonely as a cloud" he sees "a crowd, A host, of golden daffodils … Fluttering and dancing in the breeze." He takes these as a synecdoche for all of creation, since they are "Continuous as the stars that

---

3. George Herbert, "The Elixir," at http://www.poetryfoundation.org/poem/173627.

shine And twinkle on the milky way." But the important thing is that they are having their own celebration, independent of him: "Ten thousand saw I at a glance, Tossing their heads in sprightly dance." There's a whole chorus of created joy going on: "The waves beside them danced; but they Out-did the sparkling waves in glee." He paused little at the time, yet it proves the sight has changed him for good, for in moments of solitude they flash upon his inward eye: "And then my heart with pleasure fills, And dances with the daffodils."[4]

A similar experience characterizes a slightly different notion of being with the creation. In his poem "Tintern Abbey" Wordsworth returns to a place of beauty last seen five years before, and once again sees "These waters, rolling from their mountain-springs With a sweet inland murmur."[5] But he is much more aware of the effect such views have on his soul, the cliffs "Which on a wild secluded scene impress Thoughts of more deep seclusion." Even though he has long been away, Wordsworth has continued to dwell on these remembered images, and in weary and lonely moments has been stirred by "sensations sweet, Felt in the blood, and felt along the heart, And passing even into my purer mind With tranquil restoration." To these remembrances he attributes two further capacities: first, feelings "Of unremembered pleasure," such that come from true virtue, what he calls "His little, nameless, unremembered acts Of kindness and of love"; and second, "that blessed mood" which lightens the burden of the soul, and "with an eye made quiet by the power Of harmony, and the deep power of joy, We see into the life of things." Wordsworth equates this wondrous seeing with the anticipation of

4. William Wordsworth, "I Wandered Lonely as a Cloud," at http://www.poetryfoundation.org/poem/174790.
5. William Wordsworth, "Lines Composed a Few Miles above Tintern Abbey, On Revisiting the Banks of the Wye during a Tour. July 13, 1798," at http://www.poetryfoundation.org/poem/174796.

eternal life, for at such moments, he says, "we are laid asleep In body, and become a living soul."

What Wordsworth gives us here is texture for boundless delight. Wordsworth's delight in creation is truly enjoyment and exultation in it for its own sake; but he also explores how the memory of that delight comforts him in his loneliness, even his fear of death, ennobles his mundane experience, inspires and animates his gestures of generosity, and gives him an insight into the life eternal, when he will perpetually have that sense of joy and ability to "see into the life of things." Such is a more detailed account of the nature of delight. And such is a helpful account of what it means to offer the prayer of delight in a way that goes beyond the awesome wonder that considers all the works God's hand has made, beyond also the forest glades and the birds singing sweetly in the trees, and reaches the formation of the moral imagination. Wordsworth paradoxically articulates the character of wordless joy, and gives us the shape of what it means to be with the creation and pray with delight.

Thomas Traherne is the great prophet of delight. He points out that ingratitude is among the worst sins of all.

> To have blessings and to prize them is to be in Heaven; to have them and not to prize them is to be in Hell ...: To prize blessings while we have them is to enjoy them, and the effect thereof is contentation, pleasure, thanksgiving, happiness. To prize them when they are gone, envy, covetousness, repining, ingratitude, vexation, misery. But ... to ... have blessings and not to prize them is ... worse than to be in Hell. It is more vicious, and more irrational.[6]

---

6. Thomas Traherne, "Centuries of Meditations," 1.47, in *Selected Poems and Prose* (London: Penguin, 1991). Further references to particular paragraphs are in the text.

How then should we practice gratitude and embody delight? This is Traherne's favorite subject. "Your enjoyment of the world is never right," he says, "till every morning you awake in Heaven; see yourself in your Father's Palace; and look upon the skies, the earth, and the air as Celestial Joys: having such a reverend esteem of all, as if you were among the Angels" (1.28). He goes on, "You never enjoy the world aright, till the Sea itself floweth in your veins, till you are clothed with the heavens, and crowned with the stars: and perceive yourself to be the sole heir of the whole world.... Till you can sing and rejoice and delight in God, as misers do in gold, and Kings in sceptres ..." (1.29). Traherne prescribes what qualities are required to be a person who can so take delight and give thanks in all things: he says, "You never enjoy the World aright, till you see all things in it so perfectly yours, that you cannot desire them any other way: and till you are convinced that all things serve you best in their proper places.... you must have Glorious Principles implanted in your nature; a clear eye able to see afar off, a great and generous heart, apt to enjoy at any distance: a good and liberal Soul prone to delight in the felicity of all, and an infinite delight to be their Treasure" (1.38). And this is not simply about appreciating the creation around us. It is about one another and the ways of God. He goes on, "Your enjoyment is never right, till you esteem every Soul so great a treasure as our Saviour doth: and that the laws of God are sweeter than the honey and honeycomb because they command you to love them all in such perfect manner.... God commandeth you to love all like Him, because He would have you to be His Son, all them to be your riches, you to be glorious before them, and all the creatures in serving them to be your treasures, while you are His delight, like Him in beauty, and the darling of His bosom" (1.39).

Participation is being with in its simplest form, because unlike partnership it suspends awareness of different levels of skill, power, experience, or ability. The reality that faces the world today that Wordsworth did not imagine is that the fruits of the industrial revolution have seriously, indeed grievously, depleted the earth's ability to sustain itself, and that it is hard to envisage that depletion significantly slowing, let alone being reversed. While Wordsworth enjoyed the earth, most of his successors have used it. What needs to change? The theological work is in the area of participation. So much theological energy has been given to establishing and identifying ways in which humanity is distinct from the creation. Does humanity's uniqueness lie in its being able to talk, or to reason, or even, in the view of one contemporary theologian, to pray?[7] Or is humankind's uniqueness simply that God chose to be its companion and in Christ became incarnate in human form, thus singling humanity out for the bearing of the divine image? So much attention in interpreting the creation accounts focuses on humans as being made in the image of God (Gen. 1:27) and about their subduing the earth and having dominion over it (Gen. 1:28). What is lost in this emphasis is the with— humankind's being with the creation. It is as if the anxiety is always how humanity is to be with God, and the risk is that being with the creation, living as "a beast that wants discourse of reason," will somehow drag humanity away from being with God.[8] What needs recovering is the sense in which humanity is part of the creation—not first of all its owner, or controller, or conqueror, but its companion. Perhaps humanity will save the earth by being with it and becoming its companion, just as God saves humanity by becoming its companion in Jesus.

Participation with the creation thus yields confession

---

7. Robert W. Jenson, "The Praying Animal," in *Essays in Theology of Culture* (Grand Rapids: Eerdmans, 1995), 117–31.

8. *Hamlet*, Act 1, scene 2, line 152.

and lament concerning the ways humanity has used rather than enjoyed the creation, especially in the last century or more. Environmental depredation is less about what some egregious people have done somewhere and more about what humankind has come to take for granted almost everywhere. Before hastening into intercession, a disciple or congregation needs to pause and be thankful and express wonder at the many-splendoredness of creation and the privilege of humanity's being part of it. Humanity has arguably lost the moral authority to be trusted to pray for the wider creation. Thus if intercession follows, it should be from a place of being with the creation, rather than a modified form of stewardship on its behalf. And it should be accompanied by humble, concrete, and perhaps radical steps to change the way a congregation relates to fuel and other resources, and not just by demands for others to be transformed.

The notion of **partnership** is challenging to an anthropocentric view that assumes the creation is primarily or wholly there to benefit and resource humankind. In Mark 1 we read Jesus "was with the wild beasts; and the angels waited on him" (verse 13). More explicitly in 1 Kings 17, we are told of Elijah, "The ravens brought him bread and meat in the morning, and bread and meat in the evening; and he drank from the wadi" (verse 6). So there is no question that animals can work with God and human agency to further and anticipate the kingdom. As for the wider creation, human partnership with God's action, exercised through soil and sea, is the stuff of harvest hymns: God "sends the snow in winter, the warmth to swell the grain, the breezes and the sunshine, and soft refreshing rain." While human beings plow and scatter seed, that land "is fed and watered by God's almighty hand."[9] Mean-

9. Jane M. Campbell, trans., "We Plow the Fields, and Scatter," at http://www.hymnary.org/text/we_plow_the_fields_and_scatter.

while, the analogy between God's bringing of the crops to fruition and the readying of humankind for salvation is again a theme of harvest song: in the words of Henry Alford, "All the world is God's own field, fruit as praise to God we yield; wheat and tares together sown are to joy or sorrow grown; first the blade and then the ear, then the full corn shall appear; Lord of harvest, grant that we wholesome grain and pure may be."[10] Being with creation breeds humility not only that human life could not exist without the way the creation ministers to it, but also that the way creation experiences growth and harvest, life recycled for nourishment, offers a parable of how humans face their own contingency and mortality.

The irony of the ecological crisis is that, while it has been humankind's failure to be in partnership, let alone participation, with the creation that has brought the planet to the prospect of disaster, it requires an unbalanced form of partnership—with the creation doing all the "work"—for the earth to be brought back from the brink. The ecological crisis is perhaps the most obvious case imaginable of using what should be enjoyed: what needs to change is the balance between what humankind believes is for its use and what it recognizes is simply to be enjoyed. To confuse the two is the essence of sin.

In establishing partnership, a key step is identifying the partners. In relation to climate change, this is by no means a point of consensus. For many, particularly those who see global warming as a problem to be fixed, it seems the central role is for governments and corporations. This view sees the issue as largely a technological one, caused by the side effects of technological advance, and to be solved in much the same way. It's skeptical about the potential of sweeping

10. Henry Alford, "Come, Ye Thankful People, Come," at http://www.hymnary.org/text/come_ye_thankful_people_come.

cultural changes: in reality people are not going to abandon their addiction to the car, jet flight is not going to cease, those in developing countries, notably India and China, are not going to desist from desiring the same level of fossil fuel consumption that Americans and Europeans take for granted. It's pragmatic about setting timescales, identifying milestones, establishing a critical path toward a broadly similar lifestyle that has far fewer deleterious environmental consequences. While currently the enforcement mechanisms on high-polluting countries are not sufficiently binding, this approach places its confidence in the market to disinvest in carbon-reliant companies and governments to introduce policies that have an eye to long-term security. In short, the whole issue is one that can be budgeted for and managed and resolved.

Others see the question from the perspective of the global poor. Climate change is a cerebral and long-term issue for the rich and comfortable: it's a present and tangible issue for the world's poor. Those living in poorer countries, and those on the economic fringe of wealthier countries, are disproportionately affected by global warming. The irony is that these are the people least responsible for causing the ecological crisis. A 2009 report claims that already 300,000 people a year are dying from the effects of climate change—and a further four billion are affected by drought, floods, crop failures, reduced agricultural yields, the loss of low-lying lands and islands, and desertification. The danger is that all the efforts of the last two generations in poverty reduction are being undone by climate change, and that bringing more people out of poverty may exacerbate climate change. From the perspective of governments and corporations, this may look simply like another management challenge. But from the point of view of the global poor, the disproportionate cost of global warming on those who've done least to bring it about is the epitome of the injustice that lies at the heart of global trade and economic relationships. Not only have the rich despoiled their lands, but they've caused ecological crisis and then retreated to leave the poor facing that crisis alone.

A third perspective identifies the key role as one for the earth itself. Humanity constitutes the priesthood of creation, fostering and facilitating and enjoying and ordering. But the world was here before us, and it'll be here long after we're gone. We've done more damage than any previous species. But arguably the damage has been largely to ourselves. The earth will find a way to recover from the impact we've had on it, even if it takes a billion years or two: but what we do to the planet may make it impossible for our own species to survive. It's important to keep that sense of perspective. Humanity has the ability to do a lot of damage; but the earth will win out over the long term, however much damage humanity does to it. The issue for humanity is less whether there'll be a future for the planet than whether there'll be a future for itself.

Thus it emerges that the key partner is God. Climate change is not a problem *for* God: if humanity destroys the planet, or makes it uninhabitable, God is perfectly capable of creating a new planet, or a new species to be in special, incarnate relationship with. Instead, global warming is a problem that arises as an almost inevitable result of seeking a world without God. The ecological crisis, in Augustine's terms, is simply expressed: we have used what should be enjoyed. How do we learn to enjoy and not simply to use? The principal place is in worship. In worship we reorder the world so as to enjoy that which otherwise we would simply use. Every created thing has a source and a destiny: it may be a gift to us, but we should never assume that gift is our possession; rather, it's a reminder of where it came from and what purpose it serves in the kingdom. Wine comes from the grape and exists to embody Christ's blood in the Eucharist; bread comes from grain and exists to convey Christ's body. To dwell in the world in such a spirit of worship means to exult in the sheer abundance of the world and the universe beyond. It is a form of resistance to the pragmatic, bureaucratic, utilitarian culture widespread in so much human society and a celebration of the existence of things for their own sake. This should be the spirit of every act of worship: it is a joy to be alive, to be redeemed, to be a child of God, to be placed in such a great story, to live among such glorious dimensions of God's creation.

The truth is, all four of these partners are vital. The important insight of being with creation is to work one's way through them backwards. That means beginning with the sheer overwhelming joy of God and abundant delight of creation, and seeking to embody that joy and delight in our life of discipleship and ministry, with all the repentance and change of life that involves. It means then taking a sober estimate of our place in the 4 billion years of the earth's history, and neither exaggerating nor downplaying the significance of the present moment. Then we should attend to the egregious injustice that those who've done least to bring the ecological crisis about are bearing its most pressing effects. And finally, neither deterred by the purity of our worship nor overcome by the anger of our perception of injustice, we must participate in the political process of managing cultural and social change, accepting that the only argument that will prevail is that we are all doing this for our own good.

The language of participation and partnership helps clarify what's at stake in one further area: the vexed question of vegetarianism. Those who assume being with the creation means humans cannot consider eating meat pursue participation as the essence of being with. Those who believe it is justified and appropriate to eat meat regard partnership as the relevant dimension. If with is all, as for participation, eating meat is clearly out of the question; it's hard to imagine how eating an animal could be part of being with that animal. Hence people's squeamishness about eating the family cow or the domestic hen—because in such cases the with is impossible to obscure, but their relative ease in eating industrially generated meat from animals whose identity, still less personality, is entirely unknown. By contrast, partnership affirms the different roles of respective parties. In this case, those different roles mean that humans eat animals, but resist animals eating them. Animals, in this sense, are to be used rather than enjoyed. Again the domestic pet is the exception—for the family cat is to be enjoyed rather than used. To decide the issue of vegetarianism is to work out whether participation or partnership takes precedence.

As always, **enjoyment** crystallizes what it means to be with, in this case to be with the creation. Consider a pet dog. Here is presence, constant, abiding, trusting, affectionate presence. Here is attention, devoted, unwavering, perhaps a little self-interested, but nonetheless unblinking attention. Here is mystery, a creature that serves no purpose but companionship, solves no problem but loneliness, brooks no estrangement without immediate reconciliation, holds no grudge, turns to no other master, lives for no joy beyond cherishing and exercise and food. Here is delight, in the simple but abundant moments of satisfied desire, in the gamboling of the meadow and the bounding across the stream, in the diving into the lake and the thrill of chasing a ball, in the utter relish of being alive and releasing energy. Here is participation, for no walk is complete without a dog, and no dog without a walk; it seems churlish to have lunch without sharing some, unthinkable to have breakfast alone, impossible not to spend part of the day together. Here is partnership in some small way, when the guardian character of a barking puppy is welcome in a place of danger, when the warmth of a breathing companion gives succor on a cold mountain. Here is enjoyment, when a bundle of love and loyalty comes into a household with little practical purpose but, when absent or departed, is missed with a scorching wound of echoing grief. Here is glory, for when we see those sad, trusting eyes, the disciple sees the eyes of God—the eyes of the one who adores us, longs for our company, would happily spend eternity with us, forgives our every selfish betrayal, and sets aside our every doubting hesitation. We see the eyes of one who never has anything more important than us, who would give and has given anything to be our constant friend, who has little or no thought for the past but can only imagine the glorious things that lie in store for us together.

Such enjoyment in a domestic sphere discloses the nature of enjoyment in relation to God and the creation more generally. The skies, seas, and soil offer countless invitations for wonder, fulfillment, recreation, discovery, and increasingly, repentance. In this myriad of ways the creation exists to be enjoyed, and being with God and the creation, amid "Graces human and divine, Flowers of earth and buds of heaven," is a sacrament of praise.[11]

Being with the creation in a spirit of enjoyment means to exult in the sheer abundance of the world and the universe beyond. It is a form of resistance to the pragmatic, bureaucratic, utilitarian culture widespread in so much human society and a celebration of the existence of things for their own sake. This should be the spirit of every act of worship: it is a joy to be alive, to be redeemed, to be a child of God, to be placed in such a great story, to live among such glorious dimensions of God's creation. In the words of Traherne:

11. Folliott Sandford Pierpoint, "For the Beauty of the Earth," at http://www.hymnary.org/text/for_the_beauty_of_the_earth.

When things are ours in their proper places, nothing is needful but ... to enjoy them. God therefore hath made it infinitely easy to enjoy, by making everything ours.... Everything is ours that serves us in its place. The Sun serves us as much as is possible, and more than we could imagine. The Clouds and Stars minister unto us, the World surrounds us with beauty, the Air refresheth us, the Sea revives the earth and us. The Earth itself is better than gold because it produceth fruits and flowers.... By making one, and not a multitude, God evidently shewed one alone to be the end of the World and every one its enjoyer. For every one may enjoy it as much as he. (1.14)

Thus the goal of being with the creation is to enjoy the world as God enjoys it.

The last two chapters of the book of Revelation are the most vivid account of what Christians understand by **glory**. John sees "a new heaven and a new earth," and "the holy city, the new Jerusalem, coming down out of heaven from God," with "the glory of God and a radiance like a very rare jewel" (Rev. 21:1-2, 5). It turns out "the city has no need of sun or moon to shine on it, for the glory of God is its light, and its lamp is the Lamb" (verse 23). A loud voice proclaims that God will dwell with humankind as their God, and they will be God's people: being with will be the nature of God's relationship with the creation (verse 3). The city is a garden city, and John sees "the river of the water of life, bright as crystal, flowing from the throne of God and of the Lamb through the middle of the street of the city. On either side of the river is the tree of life with its twelve kinds of fruit ...; and the leaves of the tree are for the healing of the nations" (Rev. 22:1-2). Here is the fulfillment of creation with a tree proving the location of its healing as it was of its fall and its redemption. Here too is the reassembling of creation arrayed around the throne of grace. This is the climax of being with the creation: that every creature, and every element of the sentient and nonsentient creation, indeed the whole universe, find its fulfillment and its ultimate role and purpose in discovering the revelation, in whatever way attunes to their level of consciousness, that God is with them. For eternal life is being with God, with one another, and with the renewed creation, forever.

CHAPTER 4

Being with God Together

The presupposition of church is that being with one another is being with God. Church is about **presence**. It's about showing up. The pastor or priest who is told, "My thoughts are with you—I care so much about this place," and thinks in return, "But we never see you!" is entitled to suppose those pious thoughts are a mixture of sentimentality, nostalgia, and wishful thinking. Being with one another means exactly that—being present to one another, in the same place at the same time, regularly, habitually, in such a way that exercises priority over other commitments, not always, but usually, crafting one's life around the rhythm of congregational gathering, weekly, perhaps more, to worship, and no doubt again at another time for a related purpose. Sunday morning doesn't suit everyone, which is why other times are set aside for gatherings and celebrations and encounters that supplement and enhance or even replace being together for all, some of the time, and for some, all (or almost all) of the time.

Ecclesia means assembly; the church is not just for worship, but for assembling together. If this is only for worship it is inadequate, but if it is seldom or never about worship it is incoherent. A "church" names a community of persons who have come to regard being with God as being definitively practiced amid the particularities and contingencies of being with one another.

There are three kinds of gatherings to be with God and one another explicitly in prayer. The first and most obvious is a gathering to pray. To pray together means, invariably, to read scripture, to share and express needs and intercede, to articulate joy and to praise, to repent and to confess, to name causes for gratitude and to give thanks, sometimes to sing, sometimes to expound and interpret scripture, sometimes to seek healing. These things can be done casually when need demands or opportunity arises; informally to minimize preparation and ease the burden of hospitality; or formally, in an ordered, formal act of public worship that may have a published liturgy and carefully prepared music and sermon. Whatever form it takes, it affirms the principal expectation of those gathered, rooted in Jesus's promise: "Where two or three are gathered in my name, I am there among them" (Matt. 18:20). People find all kinds of reasons not to be present. Nonetheless showing up at such gatherings is the most elementary necessary-but-not-sufficient notion of church.

The second kind of gathering is to break bread and drink wine together, remembering Christ's command to "Do this in remembrance of me" (Luke 22:19). Different traditions have varying practices of the regularity of this celebration, how formal and ordered it should be, what precisely they believe takes place in the taking, blessing, breaking, and sharing, and how pivotal it is in the life of the church. But almost all traditions see in this particular gathering an embodiment of Christ's final promise, "Remember, I am with you always, to the end of the age" (Matt. 28:20), and the Bible's final crescendo, "Surely I am coming soon" (Rev. 22:20). Christians make this celebration central to their common life because they believe Christ was never more with the disciples than he was at this moment, and that he is never more with the church today than when disciples practice his command to do this in remembrance of him. Within this remembrance lie so many of the practices that constitute the church—confessing sin, being reconciled, listening to scripture, making intercession, declaring faith, giving thanks, being renewed in mission, perhaps washing feet. A Eucharist is a church in microcosm.

The third kind of gathering to pray is for a particular occasion, a beginning, like a wedding, or an ending, like a funeral; a commissioning, like the sending out of a missionary, or an invoking of the Holy Spirit, like a confirmation; a dedication, like the blessing of a new sanctuary, or a thanksgiving, like the anniversary of a ministry. Of these, the definitive act of worship is baptism. Baptism is a unique event that depicts and embodies the change that is at the heart of the church— from death to life, from sin to forgiveness, from slavery to liberation, from scarcity to abundance, from isolation to the communion of saints. It is the beginning that shapes all beginnings. It is where creation, birth, and conversion meet.

If these are the three occasions when Christians gather to pray, spontaneously or habitually, formally or informally, then there are perhaps five kinds of occasions when Christians gather for other purposes. We could call them gatherings to build up the body, to care for the weak, to resource the community, to encounter, receive from and serve the stranger, and to discern the good of the body.

Attention names the way prayerful participation in church life differs from just showing up. Attention means seeing the ordinary and the poignant moments in the life of a congregation as forms of prayer. It means being committed to perceiving both the humanity and the divinity of the church.

For example, the people gather to worship and one of the regulars is missing, perhaps more than once. On a human level this awakens a sense of pastoral care—a person who is close to the heart, or at least the heartbeat, of the community will want to contact the missing person. Is that person sick, or in trouble, or in need of care? Is that person angry or estranged or exhausted, or in some way in need of reconciliation with God or the congregation or one member of it? But there is also a divine level. If a pastor or lay representative visits that person, do they think of themselves as a good shepherd reaching the lost sheep, or as a slave fetching a buried talent out from the ground to put it back to work, or as a comforter going to sit beside Job for seven days and nights because his suffering was so great, or as an ignorant David going to be told by Nathan how he has betrayed God's trust? Attention means being aware of human dynamics like transference and passive aggression, both of which may be in evidence in such an encounter, but at the same time recalling that Jesus said "when I was sick you took care of me" (Matt. 25:36) and, referring to Zacchaeus, who was as estranged from the community as could be, "The Son of Man came to seek out and to save the lost" (Luke 19:10). Attention means holding these two dimensions together, care and prayer, and yet keeping an open mind and maintaining relaxed awareness to receive whatever discoveries and surprises this encounter has in store. On leaving the house, the visitor will ideally have prayed with the missing person—but even if not, they should still have understood the encounter as a prayer, at the very least a prayer of attention.

To give another example, attention on both levels is at work when a member of a congregation wonders whether the social and racial contours of the community healthily reflect and resemble the diversity of the population of the neighborhood. Has this congregation received everything

God has been giving it in the array of identities from which it would want to draw? Again, some of these questions are human ones—do the worship times exclude those whose work patterns seldom allow them to be present? Does the iconography of the sanctuary depict a God with a bias to a certain race or gender? Is the leadership wholly or largely drawn from a particular social location? These are conventional, largely human questions. But there are divine questions too. When the congregation reads the story of the Exodus, does it automatically identify with the Hebrews, or does it consider whether in global political terms it more closely looks like the Egyptians? When it reads Romans 13, does it assume it is a minority community that has no power in making the laws, or does it take for granted a democratic system in which it can play an active role? When it reads the Christmas story, does it concentrate on the cozy stable and the lowing oxen, or on the draconian census, murderous king, and migrating holy family? The way the congregation attends to social diversity is a form of prayer, because it relates to the way it reads the Bible. The question is, is a congregation that is not significantly characterized by those in the social locations that overwhelmingly populate the Bible capable of truly attending to the story the scriptures tell? Can such a congregation truly pray in the power of the Spirit, if it does not reflect the diversity of the church the Spirit birthed at Pentecost?

Thus attention dwells not just on who is present, but on who is not present, and who should be present. All of these are forms of confession, because each of them is a way the congregation makes itself vulnerable to being shown it is not what it is called to be, it is not yet reflecting the glorious liberty of the children of God, it has taken what was supposed to be called a house of prayer for all nations and, if not made it a den of robbers, then at least rendered it a shadow of what it was made to be. Confession in corporate worship is not just the corporate confession of personal shortcomings; it is the recognition before one another of ways the whole body has wounded others and is itself wounded by its own hand. Some of these are ways the congregation has fallen short of the standards any aspirational human organization would expect of itself; others are rooted in its calling to go beyond decency, respect, and good order and embody the fruits of the Spirit. Both of these dimensions of confession arise from attention.

The crucible of the Bible is the transformation of a colossal problem into an intriguing **mystery**. Second Isaiah describes how, languishing in Babylonian captivity, Israel realized, to its astonishment, that it was closer to God in exile that it had ever been in the Promised Land. The secret of being with God together as a praying congregation is to make the same transition. Just as intercessory prayer is not primarily about getting God to fix things but about being invited into the mystery of the Transfiguration, so congregational life is not so much about due order and positive outcomes as it is about recognizing that struggle and setback are invitations to go deeper into the heart of God.

The Gospel stories, certainly the synoptic Gospels, are arranged as a journey from Galilee to Jerusalem; and the Acts of the Apostles is set out as a journey from Jerusalem to Rome. The notion of a journey as a metaphor for life in general or the life of faith in particular is a commonplace one. More accurate is the medieval notion of the quest, by which the participants learn about themselves, about one another, and about the nature of the thing sought after: in fact they discover more about these things as they travel along the road than they do in their actual arriving.

To talk about a quest is not to assume an arrival. For Christians both the distinction between the eternal, all-powerful creator and the contingent, mortal creatures, and the notion of original sin, by which even humanity's best efforts fall short of the glory of God, make it clear that any idea of arriving is beyond the efforts of disciple or congregation. Rather than lament this, a congregation turns its life into prayer when it embraces the perspective this humble recognition brings. Few arguments are so persuasive in setting aside virtue than hurry: there is no time to lose, the goal is in sight, the opportunity will pass, the window will close, the time to strike is now—these are urgent, eager inducements to put outcome before method, end before means, urgent omelet before concern about breaking eggs. "Had we but world enough and time," as Andrew Marvell said to his mistress, "This coyness, Lady, were no crime."[1] It's urgency that proves compelling: "But at my back I always hear Time's wingèd chariot hurrying near; And yonder all before us lie Deserts of vast eternity." The recognition that we will not complete, finish, arrive, achieve turns the quest for fulfillment and lasting security into a prayer for God to fulfill that to which we have faithfully contributed. Participation is all we ask for: credit is ephemeral and glory is eschatological. There's no hurry: arrival is in God's hands alone; we cannot hasten or alter it; any proximate sense of achievement we seek is from our vanity and not for God's majesty.

This has two implications for congregational life. One is that it prevents the church taking itself too seriously. Its grandest efforts cannot bring the kingdom; its grotesque failures cannot ruin or foil the kingdom either. This is from beginning to end a story about God, in which it is our privilege to be granted a minor part. It is not for the gravedigger to upstage Hamlet: we are not the main character in the story. In the light of the incarnation the church can never downplay

1. Andrew Marvell, "To His Coy Mistress," at http://www.poetry foundation.org/poem/173954.

the validity of its ordinary and poignant moments. But the real drama of prayer lies not in invoking the Spirit to bless the Easter parade or alleviate the father-in-law's arthritis or enliven the youth group; it lies in entering the mystery of the Holy Trinity and feeling at the same time out of one's depth, unworthy, humbled, and yet welcome and glad beyond words to be there—as Jacob put it, "How awesome is this place! This is none other than the house of God, and this is the gate of heaven" (Gen. 28:17). The first business of the church is to lead people into this companionship with God, conscious of the privilege of being there, the grace of what brought them there, the joy of the fellowship they find there, and the longing to draw others there too. Being with one another is predicated on being with God. And being with God is something for which there are no adequate forms of expression: it is simply to be enjoyed, beyond compare, for its own sake.

The other implication of the mystery of God for the life of the congregation is that it makes mystery the primary perspective from which to see its initiatives and dynamics, rather than the occasion of last resort. How the congregation relates becomes more important than where it gets to. This is a vital aspect of the way new members are formed and educated and how the congregation is renewed and reoriented. The world wants to get things done and quickly move on to the next thing: it seldom pauses to cherish, to evaluate, to learn, or to acknowledge inadequacies. The church knows genuine accomplishment is rare, and there is no next thing to move on to. To enjoy its life, and see it in its entirety as prayer, takes habit and formation. Eccentric and challenging members, rather than taking up precious time, become prophets and gifts to the community. Major disputes involving arguments and harsh words, rather than delaying initiatives or discrediting integrity, become detours that lead to discovery and new perspective. Disappointments, sickness, and misadventure become opportunities to reassess expectations and recall the with and its corresponding ethic of companionship in the face of adversity. Even fragility, folly, and failure become invitations to look into the mystery of one another's longings, tenderness, and imperfection, to learn more and grow in forgiveness and reconciliation. A conventional model might suggest that we dedicate the endeavor to God, then act and achieve, and finally pause to give thanks. Mystery suggests a different model. It expects things to go wrong and for the wrong turnings to be more interesting than the seamless accomplishment would have been. It assumes that God is more fully made known in these wrong turnings than in effortless perfection. It takes for granted that repair and restoration are closer to the church's identity than creation. And its prayer is not simply, "Set things straight and make everything come out right," but "Show us a truer picture of ourselves, your kingdom, and most of all you, that through closer understanding of the poverty of our nature we may more fully comprehend the riches of your grace, and in the renewal of our lives you may make known your heavenly glory." Mystery and sacrament are the same word in different languages. The prayer of mystery induces the congregation to see every material thing in their life as a sacrament, and thus as a window into the mystery of God.

The transformed attitude to time and to achievement or arrival that characterizes the prayer of mystery also evokes the prayer of **delight**. There are two broad dimensions to delight: delight in being a child of God, and delight in being alive. Joy arises in discovering the inextricability of the two. Celebration is at the heart of every healthy community. Every year perhaps there is a festival to mark the church's foundation or the patron saint's feast day or the pastor's anniversary, and the occasion is concluded with a banquet or a dance or a contest or all three. To watch the rather solemn organist spinning the somewhat surly advocate for minority issues, to observe the understated Sunday school children's supervisor being twirled by the happy-go-lucky maintenance specialist, to witness the newly bereaved organizer of elderly care being shepherded around the floor by the nosy but caring office administrator—this is a glimpse of the kingdom's upside-down playfulness and ingenuous joy. One year perhaps a bright spark decides to rehearse a drama—maybe a largely unscripted comedy or pantomime, and a month later there are laughter and tears of hilarity as the pompous head server becomes the back end of a horse, or the sheepish and seldom-seen husband of the youth worker becomes the dashing but largely silent butler. These are the kind of activities that arise for their own sake when a community of people enjoy one another's company and find fulfillment there that they search in vain for elsewhere. They happen when people delight in being a child of God such that they cease to feel every single one of their actions has to produce lasting benefit or tangible reward, but are instead glad to throw themselves into the upbuilding of community and the selflessness of fellowship. They occur when delight in being alive becomes infectious and a congregation realizes its life is most authentic in itself and attractive to outsiders when it sheds the earnest insistence that everything be done for clear devotional or evangelistic goals and instead exults in the purposeless abundant gifts it has been given.

The most infectious expression of delight is a baby's gurgle or an infant's unstoppable laugh. To express the prayer of delight, a congregation must rediscover this unselfconscious joy and become like a little child. Of course there are cares, there is maintenance, there are finances, there is the roof, there are health and safety concerns and contracts and daily worries. But if the congregational year is not punctuated by moments of planned yet spontaneous delight, one of the most important aspects of corporate prayer is seldom if ever discovered and the life of the congregation is profoundly impoverished. Underneath all the responsibilities and beneath the carefully formed faith and practice of the church must lie a squeal of unbridled celebration, an ability to see beyond custom, rule, liturgy, process, order, and procedure, to the innocent, simple, uncomplicated wonder of wide-eyed delight. This, in the end, is how God beholds us. This is the effervescent energy behind our beholding God in return.

In any congregation there needs to be a balance between democratization that encourages everyone to **participate** and specialization that enables key tasks to be done well. It is a beautiful thing when in the course of a single act of worship a lesson from Lamentations is read by a child whose mother is seeking asylum and a lesson from 1 Corinthians about having the mind of Christ is read by a person with Alzheimer's. Such things are made possible by consideration that enables the child to stand on a platform and thus reach the microphone and by planning that prints out the reading so that if any words get missed they can be followed in a service sheet. Participation in this sense is not about widening the ministry team so that eight people do all the jobs rather than one: it's about realizing that all are called to ministry and accordingly harnessing the gifts and potential of each member to enrich the life of the whole. When a wheelchair-user serves communion, even if it means communion is served from a different place that day, or a blind person administers prayers for healing, even if it takes a companion to ensure the laying-on of hands is done deftly, what could otherwise have been a routine assignment of tasks becomes a prayer for the church to look more like the kingdom.

To achieve such a prayer is the principal goal of Christian education. Such education is constantly in search of its raison d'être. Is it intended to bring the young person or the stranger to a living faith in the God of Jesus Christ? This is catechesis. Is it designed to equip the disciple with all the available information about scripture, church history, theology, ethics, and the practices of discipleship and ministry such as spirituality, apologetics, and pastoral awareness, that they may better be able to love God and serve their neighbor? Is it best understood as the formation of character? If being with both God and one another is the telos of the church's life, then the purpose of education is to train people for participation. It would be straightforward, and not flippant, to say that means education and training in the nature and practice of presence, attention, mystery, delight, partnership, enjoyment, and glory. We have already seen that education is in part shaping the congregation's imagination to enter the mystery of God and one another, rather than solving the problems of themselves and the world. In that sense education is a kind of managing expectations, and a discovery that being with, both giving and receiving, is a different matter to the assumptions of working for. But here what we see is education in a more dynamic sense, that recognizes being with God and one another does not come easily or naturally to many people, especially those formed by an assertive, urgent, and commodifying culture. The point about participation, unlike partnership, is that it emphasizes being with for its own sake, in ways that are shared by all, whereas partnership highlights the different contributions and gifts that all can bring. Education is about developing in a whole community the qualities required to be together, sustainably, over a long period, and not just to survive but to thrive, relishing one another and the challenges life brings.

Participation is a recognition that if we're with God, and with one another, there's nothing we cannot face, endure, or be in some way enriched by. Likewise if we're not with God, and not with one another, there is little if any joy to be had.

If eternal life is being with God and one another and the renewed creation, then participation anticipates eternity and trains our imaginations for it; it loosens our desire to get to wherever we were so urgently headed, and inclines us rather to look to either side and check that our fellow passengers are on board and enjoying the ride.

Partnership refers to the particular and distinct roles of God and the disciple, or different members of the congregation, one from another. It is still about with, but more working with than simply being with. There are three kinds of prayer involved. The first is for discernment, concerning who is called to which ministry. The second is for commission, of those to different ministries. The third is of intercession, which concerns what it is apparent or transpires that only God can do.

The prayer of discernment begins with the assumption that baptism is not simply the end of the old life but the beginning of a new life in which ministry will be a defining characteristic. Therefore all are called to ministry—the only question is, to which one. Discernment distinguishes between three kinds of ministry: self, skills, and Spirit. The ministry of the *self* is the definitive ministry of being with, because it relies on no particular attributes or charisms, only the willingness to be present, attentive, aware of mystery, taking delight, and so on. For this reason it's perhaps the most important ministry, because everyone can offer it. It's also the most vulnerable ministry, because one cannot fall back on one's talents or hide behind one's specialization. A person volunteering for a lunch club for otherwise-isolated elderly people may bring culinary skills, but those could become an excuse to hide in the kitchen and avoid genuine encounter with the people the program seeks to be with. If instead the person simply offers to wait at tables, or even simply sits and eats alongside the elderly people, they are much more at the mercy of conversation and need to fit in more adeptly to the pace and expectations of lunchtime culture. Anyone can do it—but many would choose to be in the kitchen, which more nearly resembles the bustle and purposefulness of a working environment.

The ministry of *skills* is often regarded as the goal of lay participation, but it risks devolving into a working-for pattern where disciples simply replicate their professional or technical aptitudes in a congregational setting. It's marvelous to have a qualified accountant as a church treasurer, so long as the disciple doesn't assume the professional status of accountancy acquires the same seniority in a congregation as often as it would in a commercial setting, so long as the identity of accountant doesn't trump the identity of disciple, and so long as the ethos of the secular workplace informs but doesn't dominate the ethos of church. It's wonderful to have a trained teacher to do Christian education, so long as corresponding transitions are made. The danger remains that everyone simply does at church what they do elsewhere, and church feels rather more like elsewhere as a consequence. Expressed differently, the ministry of skills seems to depend less on prayer, less on grace, less on miracle, and rather more on sufficiency, competence, and adequacy.

The ministry of the *Spirit* is described rather more in the New Testament than the other ministries. Some have or develop skills in public speaking; but preaching is a gift rather than a skill—in other words it's bestowed by the Holy Spirit for the building up of the body rather than simply transferred from being honed in another context. The brilliant speaker who has nothing of the gospel to say is not a preacher. The gift of healing is not the same as the skill of physician or surgeon; healing is configured in relation to repentance, forgiveness, and reconciliation, rather than in relation to diagnosis, medication, and cure. Prophecy is not the same as prediction:

it's about being so soaked in the tradition of the scriptures and the imagination of the church and the contours of the kingdom that one can name a truth that others cannot yet perceive. These are spiritual gifts. What marks them out is that they are shaped by and useless without prayer. They are spoken, embodied, and shared prayers.

Preaching lapses into education or entertainment or instruction unless it is understood as God's address to the congregation in a prayerful conversation. The laying-on of hands becomes a technique or an amateurish form of therapy unless it's considered by all parties to be a tangible way of receiving God's response to fervent prayer. Prophecy becomes speculation or manipulation unless it is heard as a direct word from the Lord needing interpretation—a corporate experience of answered prayer. Unlike the ministry of self and of skills, these gifts are not principally about participation: they are about God meeting a congregation in its scarcity and offering it abundance. Spiritual gifts are like manna in the wilderness—they arise in a context where people fear there will not be enough, and they suffice so long as no one tries to bureaucratize or hoard them out of anxiety of their falling short. Thus they affirm the nakedness of prayer.

One significant question, within this threefold pattern of self, skills, and Spirit, is where stewardship belongs, in the narrow sense of giving or tithing money. If it's about self, then there's a simple expectation that each congregation member contributes to the costs of the common life, without assuming that contribution creates any significant say in how the money is spent. If it's about skills, then there is a clear proportionality by which the wealthier members give more than the less well-off. But the logic of skills risks that those who give more may feel they should have more say. If it's about Spirit, then giving money is about calling and discernment. This is more obviously the territory of prayer; but it runs into the constant issue of discernment in the church—when one person's idea of what God is saying differs from another's. Here is a moment when it becomes clear that being with God and one another has an authority greater than being with God alone—for self-deception, particularly in an area like money, is endemic, and the best way to counter it is through accountability to and scrutiny by a large body. The question of tithing money is revealing, because the ministry of self suggests everyone should give a regular figure—say 10 percent of income; the ministry of skills finds many reasons why this might not apply in certain cases and argues that the giving of time and aptitude should substitute or compensate for the shortfall in the giving of money; while the ministry of the Spirit recognizes that some people should be giving a lot more than 10 percent and should perhaps be thinking of the way they spend money as a spiritual gift and not just a routine form of discipleship. These are all different forms of prayer. The sin of Ananias and Sapphira was to say money is about being with God but not about being with one another; their punishment was extreme, but their error is alive and widespread.

Besides money, the other most pressing way in which partnership is expressed in congregational life is in collective decision-making. Here the threefold distinction between self, skills, and Spirit is again important. Few congregations are small enough, have enough time, and know one another well enough to make decisions as one whole body. Thus the ministry of self is not the model at work here. Once again, the key distinction is between skills and Spirit. The ministry of Spirit affirms that, through bestowal by the Holy Spirit, discernment by the congregation, and commission in an act of corporate prayer, certain members are set aside for a given period, say a year or three years, to make decisions on behalf of the whole body concerning that whole body. The point is that the ministry of skills is not the only one at work here; just because a person runs a business or a school or a branch of local government, that doesn't make them automatically well suited to steering a church. Of course their skills are welcome and may be very helpful; but they also need to be shaped by the imagination of presence, attention, mystery, delight, and so on, and the most important gifts they need are ones only the Spirit can give. Starting and ending meetings with a prayer is therefore not a routine nod to a larger context for the discussion; it is a humble recognition of where self and skill end, and Spirit must take over.

This is where intercession belongs. Prayer expresses our willingness to receive God's longing for us, while intercession articulates our longing for what God alone can give. Earlier we considered three contexts of worship: the gathering to pray, the gathering to break bread, and the gathering to mark a particular threshold. Intercession is fundamental to each one. Intercession is more about the ministry of self than about skill or Spirit, as has already been said in chapter 1. The central point here is to note that partnership in relation to being with God and one another most often names the differences of role across the diversity of the "one another." But intercession names the more significant difference between God and one another, between creator and creature. Intercession arises when the creatures have done all they can do and look to God to do the rest. Regular intercession in sunshine and rain trains the congregation to look to God not just when the fuel runs out, as it were, but when the work is begun or the patient is healthy; it's about wisdom to be guided in green pastures and beside still waters, and not just deliverance from the valley of the shadow of death.

Enjoyment is the dimension of being with that crystallizes all the foregoing ones. When you ask someone what's different about their life amid the fellowship of the congregation compared to their life elsewhere, the answer you are hoping for is, "Here I am enjoyed; elsewhere I am used." To be enjoyed is to be valued for your own sake, as you are on your birthday, rather than for what you have achieved that others envy, or for what you have that others covet, or for what you can do that others can employ, or for what you look like that others can desire, or for what you know that others can harness. Even if you have achieved little, own less, can do hardly anything, look bland or worse, and have forgotten everything you knew, you can still be enjoyed. To say "Here I am enjoyed" is to say "Here people are present to me, attentive to me, appreciate the mystery of me without trying to fix me, take delight in and with me, look to participate with me, share in partnership the things I can contribute and the things others are better suited or able to bring, and all for the glory of God." To put it another way, it is to say "Here my life becomes a prayer; here I know what it means to be enjoyed by God; here I glimpse the forgiveness that redeems my past and the eternal life that characterizes my future; and here I am moved to enjoy God and others in return."

Churches can be many things other than church. A network of churches across a relatively under-resourced part of the world can be a perfect channel for healthcare, education, and community development. A close-knit denomination of churches across an oppressed nation can be a unique focus for nonviolent resistance, alternative assembly, and the funneling of refugees. A vibrant congregation with many single people can be a wonderful place to meet a spouse or for a young parent to find a babysitter or a property agent to sell a house. In beneficial, benign, and less admirable ways such activities go on in churches around the world every day. But they are all forms of using rather than enjoying. That doesn't make them wrong; but it names the way they fall short of worshiping and enjoying God forever. Mission names the ways in which the church enjoys the world; but to be the church Christians must first and foremost enjoy God and, in enjoying God, enjoy one another. The church exists for prayer, and prayer is fundamentally people coming together to enjoy God enjoying them.

Glory is the purpose of all things. The key point is that glory is a collective experience and is inherently entered as prayer. In a human context, the term "glory" is used as an exclusive category, reserved for those of exceptional military, athletic, or otherwise public dignity or achievement—coined as a way of capturing widespread acclaim or notable victory and seeking to describe it in terms that overcome life's ephemerality and make it permanent. But heavenly glory, being with God forever, is not an exclusive notion. It is for the whole company of heaven—angels and archangels, cherubim and seraphim, saints and martyrs, and the most humble of God's creations. The requirement, echoing the parable of the talents, is that you receive God's grace and turn it into praise. All prayer, in the end, is preparation for and anticipation of glory—the gathering around the throne of grace. Being with God alone cannot be our final destiny. In heaven, we are gathered with God and one another. And our prayer is transformed into praise.

CHAPTER 5

Being with Child

There's a significant overlap between discipleship and ministry. At the simplest level, straightforward acts of kindness are on the borderline between the two: a car has a flat battery, and a fellow church member asks you to draw your car alongside to recharge her car from yours. This is discipleship, because it's uncomplicated kindness; but it's ministry, because it's a practical act of mercy. At a more sophisticated level, when a church community gathers for worship, there's a gray area between what people are doing out of discipleship—humbly following Jesus—and what could better be called ministry—taking on formal or informal roles in building up the body. For example, when a person greets another at the church door it's an act of discipleship; when that same person puts on a badge and becomes an assigned Greeter then it becomes ministry. Overseeing a church is in large part about ensuring the collaboration and comprehensiveness of the latter without losing the spontaneity and genuineness of the former.

Perhaps the most intriguing overlap lies in what it means to be a parent, and, to a slightly lesser degree, what it means to be a child.[1] I say to a lesser degree because a child is a child whether in relationship to a parent or not; but a parent (as compared to an adult) is defined by their relationship to a child. Hence part of the agony of having your child die before you do, especially if it's your only child: Are you then still a parent, if you have no child? Whereas you can still be a child even if you have no parents. Likewise the sadness and complexity of feeling called to be a parent yet never oneself having a child. Meanwhile, any adopted child knows the complex interweaving of biological, moral, and role-shaped qualities involved in the notion of parent: Is one a parent by simply fertilizing an egg, whether *in utero* or *in vitro*, intentionally, unintentionally, or as a donor; by giving birth; by being a caring, nurturing, loving presence; or by being a regular, at-least-largely responsible adult in the home?

So a parent is a moral designation; but not only or always so. Jesus redefines parenthood and other relations in his words "Whoever does the will of God is my brother and sister and mother" (Mark 3:35). And being a child is elevated to a moral status by Jesus's words in the Gospels: "It is to such as these that the kingdom of heaven belongs" (Matt. 19:14); "Unless you change and become like children, you will never enter the kingdom of heaven. Whoever becomes humble like this child is the greatest in the kingdom of heaven. Whoever welcomes one such child in my name welcomes me" (Matt. 18:2-5). Thus the role of parent as all-knowing, totally responsible mediator of the complex world to the innocent child—distiller of wisdom, teacher of habits and morals, protector from storms and evils—such a status is undermined and subverted by Jesus's exaltation of the child

---

1. Recent helpful reflections on parenthood and ministry include Emma Percy, *Mothering as a Metaphor for Ministry* (Farnham, UK: Ashgate, 2014), and Elizabeth O'Donnell Gandolfo, *The Power and Vulnerability of Love: A Theological Anthropology* (Minneapolis: Fortress, 2015).

and its privileged access to and perspective on the kingdom. "The Child is the Father of the Man": Wordsworth's words, the capital letters hinting at a Trinitarian dimension, affirm the priority of childhood, not just in terms of human lifespan and character formation, but also morally and epistemically.[2] In short, children teach their parents—about life, about God, about themselves, about parenting.

So being with child challenges the distinction between discipleship and ministry; and it subverts the conventional portrayal of the parent's superiority over the child. But there's a third dimension that this chapter seeks also to explore—and it's contained in the mysterious and intriguing expression, "being with child." For a mother, conceiving, carrying, giving birth, and breastfeeding are a unique, and perhaps definitive, experience of the ministry of being with. These are things a father can enjoy and behold and support; but a father's ministry, while important, requires a different kind of being with.

Thus being with child invites reflection on the nature of ministry, on the nature of childhood, and the nature of bringing a child into being.

The place to begin is with **mystery**. The simplest, most earthy, primal, and physiological dimension of human existence—procreation, the propagation of the species—is also the most wondrous, tender, intimate, complex, mysterious, and fraught aspect of living. Marriage is a social and, to some extent, ecclesial attempt to harness and corral the free spirits of loneliness and desire, neediness and longing, within the established roles of spouse and parent. In its combination of mundane and fragile humanity with creative and loving

---

2. William Wordsworth, "Ode: Intimations of Immortality from Recollections of Early Childhood," at http://www.poetryfoundation .org/poem/174805.

divinity, marriage is inevitably a source of comparison with the divine and human Christ, and Christ's body, the church. More pertinent to our concern for the ministry of being with, marriage is a long-term exercise in being with, where working for and working with can both be apt extensions of, and yet risk becoming overt substitutes or subtle distractions from, being with.

In a marriage, quasi-marriage, undefined relationship, or brief encounter can come about the intimacy, sometimes profound, passionate, tender, sometimes exploitative, casual, or clumsy (in other words sometimes truly and gloriously with, sometimes scarcely or not at all) from which issues the mystery of conception. And out of this much-longed-for or deeply feared, planned and managed or ignored and neglected moment can arise, for a woman, often before she knows it, the state of being with child. This resonant phrase rewards gentle pondering. The three words amplify and clarify one another. "Being with" we have explored exhaustively: but does "child" add a rich, limitless, perhaps definitive context to being with? "Child" of course can mean zygote, embryo, or fetus; newborn, infant, or toddler; pre-teen, adolescent, or adult: to call someone a child is to note that they are contingent, hint that they are dependent, suggest that they are loved, imply that they are still growing and learning, perhaps allege that they are immature or irresponsible. Thus to try to love a person who's being cruel to one, one can recall that once they were someone's fragile child; meanwhile, to come to terms with the humanity of an admired person who turns out to have feet of clay, one can recognize that deep inside they are still a child, searching clumsily for love and security. In each case, the word "child" enriches the outlook of being with.

Likewise "being a child" turns one's attention on oneself: one never stops being a child, for, despite Paul's words, there's more to childhood than foolish things. Here "child" means that we didn't bring ourselves into the world; we have no right to be here; we have no entitlement, have made no original request, had no choice over the circumstances of our birth and early years; despite our best efforts to make ourselves freely choosing autonomous individuals, we're a child in the face of health, weather, and so much besides; and yet, paradoxically, and echoing Jesus's words, maturity lies in realizing, accepting, inhabiting, and enjoying these unalterable and ultimately overwhelming aspects of our perpetual childhood.

Leonard Wilson was an Anglican bishop in Singapore during the Second World War. When the Japanese invaded he was interned. For many months he suffered regular beatings and torture. He constantly prayed to God for patience, for courage, and for love. God gave him plenty of opportunities to exercise such virtues. In the middle of the torture his Japanese guards asked him if he still believed in God. He said, "I do." So they asked, "Why doesn't your God save you?" Bishop Wilson said, "God does save me. He doesn't save me by freeing me from pain or punishment, but he saves me by giving me the strength to bear it." Day after day, Bishop Wilson had to cower in the face of his persecutors. Many times he prayed, "Father, I know these men are doing their duty. Help them to see that I am innocent." Yet he looked at their faces as they stood round, taking it in turns to flog him, and their faces were hard and cruel, and some of them were evidently enjoying themselves. But Wilson saw them as they had been, as little children with their brothers and sisters— happy in their parents' love. He saw them not as they were, but as they were capable of becoming—and that stopped him from hating them.[3]

3. See John Bowker, *Problems of Suffering in the Religions of the World* (Cambridge: Cambridge University Press, 1970), 96-98.

Perhaps most challengingly, "with child" begs the question of whether the default preposition of adults relating to children is truly "with." Because with implies **participation**, and participation implies some kind of parity of esteem—in a way that prepositions like "for," "to," or "from"—let alone "on behalf of" or "for the sake of"—do not. Thus what the question provokes is whether adults conventionally regard a child as their equal—as having different perspectives, just as valid; unique insight, at least as, if not more acute; and profound qualities, such as wonder, that an adult might be much the poorer for having neglected or utterly lost—or adults take for granted that not just the power, but also the wisdom, experience, knowledge, strength, and responsibility lie entirely on their side, and the transfer of information and understanding is entirely one way. The phrase "with child" challenges such assumptions. It suggests "with" is the primary way one should imagine relating to a child, and holds up to examination a myriad of other ways, such as bringing up, rearing, or raising. And it suggests "child" has important, vital, perhaps uniquely significant characteristics to qualify the word "with."

Which brings us back to the mystery of what it means for a woman to be pregnant, and to describe that pregnancy as "being with child." Because here the "with" plays down the woman's agency: she isn't generating, producing, forming, or constructing a child—she is "being with" child. Even the conventional alternative expressions, such as "expecting a baby," or even the somewhat quaint "in the family way," carry a similar ambivalence or reserve about agency. And the reticence is absolutely appropriate: the woman gives everything—her energy, appetite, and shapeliness, her mobility, strength, steadiness of stomach, and quietude of head, let alone the prospect of often agonizing delivery; and yet she literally doesn't know what she's doing. The process by which

zygote becomes embryo and embryo becomes fetus happens
without her intervention, direction, or control. Matthew's account of the birth of Jesus begins with the word "genesis":
"Now the birth (lit. 'genesis') of Jesus the Messiah took place
in this way" (Matt. 1:18). It highlights the fact that a woman
has no more power to turn a zygote into a fetus than she has
to create the world: both are miracles, and mysteries. The an-
nunciation to Mary is sometimes spoken of as an egregious
invasion of her body by the Holy Spirit; but every pregnancy
is a mysterious series of events, largely, with the exception
of the conception itself, beyond the woman's control. Being
with child means, for a woman, having little more direction
of the formation of the child than the child has itself. Little
wonder we have such poignant reflections in Psalm 139:
"For it was you who formed my inward parts; you knit me
together in my mother's womb. I praise you, for I am fearfully
and wonderfully made" (verses 13-14). The father and mother
together may have planted; the mother certainly watered; but
God gave the growth. Even in cases of assisted conception,
where interventions have taken place to bring fertilization
about in vitro or facilitate it in utero, there's little or nothing
that assists or explains, once conception and implantation
have taken place, what it truly involves to be with child.

A similar, and equally moving, dynamic can take place in
the mystery of breastfeeding. Often the production of milk
can be challenging, the flow not straightforward, the significant areas prone to soreness, the newborn baby fitful and
clumsy in sensing and satisfying hunger. Like pregnancy,
much can be distressing, uncomfortable, disorienting, and
exasperating. But like pregnancy, breastfeeding is something
a mother does with, not simply for, her child. The precious
and beautiful harmony of mother and child, feeding and being fed, is a mysterious **partnership**. The effort, and the reward, is not one-way. The roles are different: but each party

teaches, trains, and enjoys the other. It's a wondrous thing to find oneself deeply, truly, and thoroughly able to satisfy another's need; it's a precious thing to have one's needs so utterly, fully, and comprehensively satisfied—with just a burp to indicate contentment. Few, if any, partnerships, when successful, are so unambiguously rewarding. Like all the best partnerships, there seems to be at work something beyond the skills and needs and desires of the respective parties: there's an unseen force that binds and teaches, harmonizes and dovetails, trains and completes, entertains and reciprocates. Who is bestowing a privilege upon whom? For which party is this the more defining experience of life? In whose soul will this pre-verbal, primal activity lodge the more irreplaceably and unmovably? For both parties the activity of transferring milk could probably be done more efficiently and speedily; but, as is the essence of with, that would be to miss the point: the point is that this is something definitively done together; efficiency and haste diminish the with that is the purpose of existence, of relationship—the **glory** of God.

Of course there's a lot of for in parenting—especially parenting a newborn. There are relentless diapers to change, equipment to prepare, clothes to wash, pacifying and soothing techniques to hone and implement with greater or lesser success; for a parent who rises often in the middle of the night the sense of mutuality may seem fantastical or sentimental; sense of humor can be an early casualty. Indeed, for many, parenting seems like the ultimate experience of working for, as life becomes a constant stream of washing, tidying, cleaning, mollifying, feeding, sterilizing, transporting, entertaining. It can seem like a blur of give, give, give. But as in marriage, the sometimes overwhelming demands of for can become an avoidance of, or at least a distraction from, the deeper invitation to with. Because, as in pregnancy, the real, profound, and constant changes—the growth, discovery, learning, exploration—aren't achieved or bestowed by the parent; they just come. Again, God gives the growth. A child's maturing is a thing of wonder—a thoroughbred horse on which the parent is at best an attentive rider. The parent who seeks the credit or claims compensatory acknowledgment for their labors or infant-management is missing the bigger part of the deal: some force is acting in, through, and with the growing child—a force with its own momentum, own wisdom, own creativity, pace, dynamic, and character; such that any parent that seeks to control, bridle, or harness it is a prisoner of their own fears and a fool in their own hubris. Parents don't fundamentally "bring their child up"; they walk with their child as that child learns through practice, failure, patience, experimentation, persistence, reflection, and discovery—qualities required of the parent as much as the child. It's a with story, from beginning to end. Being with child doesn't end at birth; it's only just begun.

And this is where **attention** becomes so vital. A problem can be solved by applying a solution learned from and applied elsewhere; a mystery can only be entered, and requires a response that draws on deep experience, but is new to this unique situation. Being with child is a mystery and not a problem. Wisdom comes primarily from close attention to this child, with this parent, in this context; advice and child-rearing manuals have their place, but only insofar as they encourage close attention to the details and particularities of this narrative. It's not a generic issue to be fixed; it's a unique story to be lived. Parenting is not a calling or ministry you can get right at, say, infancy, after which you keep doing the same thing with predictable, reliable, and positive results. The child grows. You are called to be with them. Not to make them, shape them, instruct them, train them; but neither to neglect the respective roles in the partnership, where you have a regard for their ignorance, innocence, ingenuousness, vulnerability, fallibility, and impetuousness. Instead, the parental way to be with is to pay attention: to observe, remember, enquire, be curious, encourage, wonder, respond, reflect, remind, acknowledge, thank, appreciate. There's no moment to repose in expertise or recline in having mastered this stage of life: in no time all has changed, and only the one who's truly with will perceive the change as it dawns.

And this is where the parent has to make a very significant choice: Will they take the for approach of lamenting the burden of bearing the unexpected, unwanted, ungrateful, or the with approach of **delight** toward the challenging, stretching, and surprising? The choice isn't always so stark; but to be truly with, attention, so as not to be crushing and suffocating, must elicit delight. And, just as in infancy, arguably even in the womb, the central feature of delight is the way the child is, as much as the parent, the teacher. It's a commonplace to hear a person say, "That's why we have grandchildren—to teach us how to use our phones and computers." But the truth is, even before the days of rapidly upgrading personal communications technology, it has always been so. The child has always been the father of the man in speed, agility, hearing, sight; but the child also has the gift of fresh eyes, unafraid questions, uninhibited enthusiasm, unalloyed adventure, unsullied idealism, unqualified loyalty. To discover that your child is your teacher isn't an occasion for humiliation, humor, or accusations of hubris; it's not a crossing of the bar, a time to hand over the reins, or a sign that your number is up: it's an occasion for delight, joy, happiness—and of looking back to see it has always been so. Ever since the cradle, this child has been teaching its parents what it means to be alive, to learn, to grow, to be a child of God.

There's a well-known story about the pastor who was walking home from church and passed a gardener laying out rows of vegetables in an immaculate line. "That's a beautiful garden you've got there," said the pastor. "I'm glad you like it," replied the gardener; "I've worked hard on it all these years." Quickly the pastor chimed in, piously, "You should give glory to God—for it was God who sent the rain and sun and enriched the soil and gave the growth." "Ah yes," the gardener responded; "but you should have seen what it looked like when God was working on it without my help." This is a story about delight, attention, and partnership. Indeed there is a role for the parent as this kind of gardener, giving care and nurture while God gives the growth; but a child is not a vegetable, and the real delight comes when the child brings something that wasn't already there—something perhaps not immediately wonderful or even welcome, but nonetheless a thing of wonder. It's easy to be touched by a baby's first smile, an infant's first word, a toddler's first step; but just as significant is when a child says, "If I'm not supposed to swear, why do you?"; "If you don't like soggy carrots, why do you always put so much water in the pan?"; "I go to school with lots of different kinds of people; but why do all the people you invite to our home look like us?"

Part of delight, and part of partnership, is the recognition that, while called to be with your child, your child has needs, aptitudes, and joys that require learning, discovery, and play with people other than you. Being with child, after birth, doesn't mean being inseparable from child; it doesn't mean making child wholly dependent on you; nor does it mean your becoming incapable of finding identity except in the role of parent. With is not possessive; it's not arrogant or consumed by its own needs; it doesn't insist its way is the only way. It sees being with child as an invitation to wider relationship rather than a stockade against the cruel and duplicitous outside world. Just as a parent needs to learn and grow from other adults, and from other children, so does a child. Delight, in short, is not trying to turn a child into a clone, a client, or a creation of oneself, but enjoying the child becoming a unique, surprising creation of God, church, and kingdom. And that's why it's been necessary to withhold premature discussion of **presence**.

The ministry of being with usually begins with presence. But presence means something different when it comes to discipleship—particularly discipleship that centers on the home. Parenthood, as we've seen, isn't simply biological procreation but a moral status and a vocational role—and for that latter role presence is clearly required. But parenthood comes to be as much about letting go as about being always there, as much about expressing trust and love by giving space as about offering protection and supervision by remaining in proximity. And this is never more the case than when it comes to giving emotional permission and physical breathing room for children to make a relationship and start a family of their own. So presence—while foundational to the ministry of being with more generally, and inextricable from being with child in pregnancy and often in immediate infancy—can become more complex, and even problematic, in later years.

But presence takes on a different character when one considers that it takes a church to raise a child. A congregation is an almost-unique environment where people of all ages interact in largely informal ways, and relationships can grow up naturally across family, race, and class backgrounds. Of course there are lurking dangers; but a congregation has the potential to be a source of significant relationships that put the intensity of the nuclear family in perspective and offer alternatives for nurture, mentoring, and imitation. There are many important relationships beyond parent-child: grandparent, uncle or aunt, and godparent are in many cases salvific, or at least highly salutary; fellow disciple or Sunday school teacher are spheres of great potential.

The best way to summarize the ministry of being with child is to consider it as **enjoyment**. Having children discloses the core of existence and of discipleship. It's not, as "nature" might suggest, about the survival of the species, let alone the fittest—although in subsistence economies, it may be about life insurance for those anxious about care in their advanced years. Neither is it, as a fearful ethic might suppose, about populating the world with at least an equivalent, perhaps increased, number of Christians—since the church grows through conversion and baptism, rather than conception and birth. It's not a selfless act of giving others life, in recognition that one's own life is fragile and failing, or a bland hope that one's children will make a better world than one's own and previous generations have done. And it's not about creating a small empire over which to (aspire to) exercise complete control. Being with child is to allow oneself to be drawn into a process of creation, a narrative whose course one quickly discovers to be outside one's control and beyond one's imagination; to find all one's relationships affected by the new presence, its smallness in inverse proportion to its capacity to move, inspire, infuriate, hold to ransom, transform. It's inevitably to generate countless projections, transferences, and soon-to-be-thwarted narratives of dreams fulfilled, failures reversed, ideals realized. It's to revise one's assumptions about the self—initially a part of another's body, then wholly contained within and dependent upon another, then separate but inseparable from another, then tied up with another but relating to others, then forming an independent sense of self, then by turns constantly wishing to be dependent and inseparable or again separate and self-sufficient. It foils all attempts to be used: it can only be enjoyed.

Thus being with child is an intense, complex, conflicted, and yet widespread case of the ministry of being with. More than perhaps any other sphere, it highlights the ultimate inextricability of discipleship and ministry. In the traditional English breakfast of bacon and egg, the chicken is involved by contributing the egg while the pig is committed by providing the bacon. Being with child is a poignant reminder that being with may look like the work of a chicken, but may turn out to be closer to that of a pig. Being with is not something that can be done at arm's length, simply be put down to resume another activity, be forgotten entirely and resumed the next morning: in this sense pregnancy is an apt template. If any should see ministry as the exercise of skill, discipline, and aptitude, they should reflect on the wonder of being with child—the mystery of gestation, symbiosis, formation, development, all of which are well outside and beyond expertise or honed habit. Being with means being present in awe as God gives the growth. If any should see ministry as following an established curriculum of education, instruction, devotion, and empowerment, they should reflect on the more-or-less ordered chaos of being with child. Entering into God's business of creation is seldom tidy, predictable, or malleable into an ordered pattern. Instead the ministry of being with is almost always faithful improvisation. If any should see ministry as something that can be performed with "one hand," while multitasking elsewhere, being with child is an indication that the most important things in life require two hands, full attention—and only thus yield true delight.

Above all, being with child highlights that the ministry of being with requires one's whole body, one's whole mind, and one's whole soul: like being with child, it takes one to the deepest recognition of one's earthy physicality, its beauty and clumsiness, its creativity and intractability; it takes one to the furthest reaches of thought, the wonder yet fraughtness of conception, the fears about security of relationship, health, and financial well-being, the scrutiny of development, sickness, so-called normality; it takes one to the most profound territory of faith—creation and incarnation, providence and anthropology, fall and redemption. The ministry of being with is always the ministry of Mary—being alongside the Christ child, both caring in the midst of vulnerability and standing in awe of divinity, anxious that one is unworthy to be so close to, so trusted with, so touched by the mystery, and yet realizing that somehow, in ways beyond one's own desiring, deserving, or comprehending, one has brought forth the fruit of the Spirit and beheld its glory.

CHAPTER 6

Being with the Called

All are called. All are called to discipleship; all are called to ministry; all are called to mission. In other words (to take things out of our usual sequence) **participation** is the first thing to say about calling. And all means not just every race, and gender, and class—but every age and mental/physical ability too. The question of vocation arises at every stage of life, from childhood to dotage. But not all are called to the same expression of discipleship, the same form of ministry, the same field of mission. One of the most significant fruits of being with is discernment—and that's what this chapter is about. Discernment isn't always or even usually the wise words of a thoughtful counselor at the end of a profound conversation. More often the wisdom emerges in the heart of disciples themselves, without specific articulation by another; but the accountability to and companionship of another is invariably a stimulus to reflection and a catalyst for clarity. Companions can't give hope: but they can ask for reasons for the hope that is already there.

Baptism is the departure point for discipleship, ministry, and mission. It names and enacts the difference between what we are and what we're called to be. For everyone present, it reiterates the question, "Is what you are currently about arising from your creation, or your new creation?" On the one hand, baptism is about participation, because it's the same for everybody: all undergo the stripping of bad habits, inveterate sins, and obsolete identities; all share the cleansing of water and the expression of faith; all know the reclothing in body, mind, and spirit and the sending forth as a carrier rather than a burden. But baptism is also about **partnership**. It's the definitive moment of the discernment of diverging callings: for one, discipleship is going to be almost all-consuming, and ministry and mission more general; for another, a particular ministry makes a specific demand on a disciple and perhaps a household, and most discipleship and ministry will be seen through that lens; for a third, the field of mission is unique and compelling, and discipleship and ministry fit in around it.

Thus in the first such case, perhaps a person is in prison serving a long sentence, and ministry to fellow Christians is limited, mission to the wider world almost impossible; but through daily practices of faithful discipleship, of fasting, intercession, confession, and praise, that person can sense the joy of an answered call. Or in the second case, perhaps a woman in mid-life is called to become the principal of a residential secondary or high school, and she needs not only to see her calling as one of 365-days-a-year ministry to the pupils, their parents and families, the staff, the former pupils, and the neighborhood, but also to ask her household to respond to that calling with support and participation. Or again, perhaps a man responds to a period of interreligious tension by going to live in a neighborhood or region in which Christians are few, seeking to witness to peaceable presence and make alliances and partnerships based on enjoying the community without specifically expecting to change it. In such a setting, ministry—the building up of the church—has few outlets; all is mission, the encounter with the world.

What matters is that disciples never forget for a moment that their calling is always a partnership between themselves and God, and between themselves and one another. What that means is that, while discipleship is very seldom the limit of calling, it must always be at its heart. Put differently, one's calling to be God's companion is always the subtext of one's vocation to ministry in the church or mission in the world. Meanwhile, it also means that no one has a vantage point from which to decree that one calling is higher than another. Ministry is not simply subservient and preparatory to mission. Mission is not simply a subsequent step and a recruitment ground for ministry. It's a genuine partnership: building up the church and encountering God in the world, both grounded in walking with God in the cool of the day.

One young seminarian found himself, at the end of his first year at seminary, a man in a hurry. As an undergraduate he'd been exasperated by the irrelevance of his course of study, obsessed by the need to share the gospel and tackle issues of poverty, and longing to be in a place where he could do both at the same time. Theological training, for him, was like being a soldier cooped up in a ship crossing the Channel to France in June 1944, like a coiled spring waiting to be unleashed on D-Day. So a ten-day gospel mission to a lower-middle-class parish in the summer of his first year at seminary was an opportunity to vent his energy and frustration on an unsuspecting populace. The ten students who shared the mission together with him humored his restlessness and intensity. Halfway through, he led a weekend away for the youth group. Coming back from the weekend he continued to pour his energy into the mission. At evening prayer on the Tuesday there was a long time of silence and after a few minutes he found himself sobbing. He was so worn out he had nothing emotionally or physically left. It was a little embarrassing for his colleagues, so, being Anglicans, they said a blessing and edged out of the church. The staff leader of the mission remained behind, perceiving that there wasn't much wrong besides exhaustion and a rather impoverished theology. But his words resonated for decades afterwards. "Your first duty as a priest is to save your own soul." Discipleship is prior to, and foundational for, ministry and mission.

The young seminarian's theological mistake lay in believing that his own sacrifice took away sins and redeemed the world, rather than Jesus's. His error was to believe he was ultimately accountable to the youth group and the person leading the mission. But he wasn't. He was ultimately accountable to God, for whether he'd repented and accepted forgiveness and received and embodied the Christian faith and kept the promises of his baptism and used the gifts of the Holy Spirit affirmed in his confirmation. His further error was to believe that sacrificial efforts in ministry and mission could compensate for deficiencies in discipleship. Such efforts are an attempt to be with the church and the world without being with God. Such practice is understandable, widespread—and wrong: it's the view of the third slave who knew his master to be a harsh man (Matt. 25:24), and of the one who gained the whole world but lost her soul (Matt. 16:26).

While baptism, or reflection on one's baptism, is the definitive moment for discernment, pondering and responding to one's call is a lifelong adventure. Few can say that vocation is a once-for-all thing. As is often said, the way to provoke divine laughter is to tell God your plans. Vocation is more about improvisatory response to unforeseen circumstances than a life-plan sketched in one's formative years on the back of an envelope. When it comes to being with people, the secret is to be **present** to them at such crucial turning points in their lives.

American churches take minivan groups of young people on mission trips to impoverished, exotic, or challenging destinations not to bring affluence in the face of scarcity, nor to export expertise to a land of ignorance, nor even to instill in the youth care for those less fortunate—but to facilitate conversations between participants, leaders, and local people, interactions with one another that dig into and ruminate upon deep self-examination in the face of jarring difference, unaccustomed roles, problems that have few if any answers, and the broadening experience of travel. Mission trips are simply exercises in discernment for those who make them; they are opportunities par excellence to be with people in times of reflection on social and personal interfaces of dislocation, injustice, and sometimes despair; any positive effect they may have on the hosts is a bonus.

For the same reason, chaplaincy has long been a regular feature of life in schools and hospitals. Chaplaincy is precisely about showing up and hanging about in places where transformation happens. A hospital is a place of joy and desperation, of agony and relief, of skill and powerlessness, of restoration and loss, of rapid action and patient waiting. Being with in such contexts often means the humble arts of becoming or remaining present, as outlined elsewhere in this book; but it can also mean seeking to be present, intentionally, because one expects such moments to be revelatory for a sense of vocation. The physician, after years of seeking to provide answers and solutions, begins to sense a call to listen and talk rather than examine and assess—to sit patiently on the bed, rather than stand busily beside it. The fretful daughter, waiting beside her mother's critical bed in the emergency room, notices the detailed care of the acute nurse and wonders if such might be the life for her. The recovering transplant patient, overwhelmed with relief and gratitude, makes resolutions to live differently, give without ceasing, support those similarly endangered. In all such cases the nonanxious presence of a sympathetic other can catalyze an epiphany in which calling is heard, consequences are weighed, losses are acknowledged, truth is affirmed. For the ministry of being with, a hospital is only secondarily a place of healing: it's first a site of discovery, revelation, unveiling.

Likewise at a school, college, or university, the stated purpose of all endeavor is education, and perhaps research or training. But for the ministry of being with, this is simply another rarefied location for calling and discernment. Education is a time for realizing new dimensions of truth, new ways of learning, and recalibrating one's outlook on life and one's situation in relation to all one has newly apprehended. Such discovery is bound to alter relationships and bring one into the company of the likeminded and the opposed, the attractive and the disturbing. What is my place in this world that is being unveiled before me? That vocational question is pressing in the midst of education more than perhaps anywhere else. The heart of ministry is not to introduce such a question but to be present when such a question arises of its own accord.

If the Christian life is largely made up of discipleship, ministry, and mission, being with means showing up in all three contexts. When a priest or pastor sees people largely or entirely within the confines of the church building, the underlying message is that ministry—and the particular part likely to be exercised within the confines of the church building—is the only part that really counts, or is at least the only part of interest. The primary, though by no means the only, sphere of discipleship is the home, and the principal, though certainly not the sole, field of mission is the place of work or study: being present means showing up in such places, to the extent possible and appropriate. Such presence is an incarnate statement that "God is in this place"; but it's also a vocational question—is this a tax collector's counting booth that a contemporary Levi is being called to leave (Mark 2:14), or is it a centurion's leadership in which faith, the like of which has never, even in Israel, been found, can grow (Luke 7:9)? A visit to a home can disclose the dynamics, the tensions, and the vocational questions in the assiduous activity of Martha and the wholehearted focus of Mary; the hospitality of Abraham and the hidden laughter of Sarah.

A new pair of eyes makes the house-proud prepare, but inevitably provokes questions: "Whose face is in that photograph on the mantelpiece?" "Did that chair always belong in your family, or was it a gift?" "Did you paint that still life?" Such questions, innocent as they sound, stand at the entry point to deep caverns of narrative; and vocational questions about the future invariably arise from tender moments in the past. The scrutiny of one used to making judgments in another setting can evoke defensiveness, embarrassment, shyness, or flamboyance in a working context. But again, questions automatically surface: "So where—between sourcing materials, producing goods, paying staff, marketing products, and making sales—do you actually make your profit?" "What makes you proud about this organization?" "What would you change if you were the boss?" "Are you more tempted to stay at work longer than you're paid to, or to leave earlier than you should?" Such questions have a power when uttered in the context of presence. They may be heard as Jesus saying, "Other seeds fell on good soil and brought forth grain" (Matt. 13:8)—or they may sound rather more like God asking, "What are you doing here, Elijah?" (1 Kings 19:9). The ministry of presence may mean that all that's required is to show up and ask the question: the Holy Spirit will do the rest.

As ever, when presence yields **attention**, being with turns from the general to the particular. Presence is the assurance of incarnational validity—that ordinary life in all its complexity yet quotidian mundanity is the experience Jesus inhabited for 90 percent of his earthly existence, is blessed and honored by God, and worthy of pursuing for its own sake. But attention asks one question above all others: Is this moment of your life a time of Nazareth, of abiding and growing and enjoying and cherishing? Is it a time of Galilee, of following, of transformative adventure and witnessing change, of learning the arts of community and taking risks of faith, of leaving behind the known and the good, out of a calling to the new and the hopeful? Or is it a time of Jerusalem, a unique moment of truth, sacrifice, danger—a moment that perhaps all your previous life can be seen as preparing for, the goal to which all your unclear and unrewarding seasons can now be disclosed as resourcing, a chapter that may be your last, yet best?

About this vital question (or series of questions), some things may be highlighted. The question about Nazareth takes away the assumption that all of life can and should be Nazareth. Jesus's long season in Nazareth affirms his desire to be with us above and before and beyond any other kind of relating to us. But Nazareth, as the subsequent Gospel stories set there demonstrate, was not a mill-pond of harmony and affirmation; neither did Jesus remain there permanently. Life, let alone calling, can't—and shouldn't—be entirely about organic growth, reassuring relationships, and reliable community. The question about Galilee assumes that a significant part of every life, and the defining part of many lives, is about challenge, testing, temptation, opposition, teamwork, loyalty, discovery, and being stretched. One of the key points of discernment is to what extent that vocation becomes the shared vocation of other people among household and fellowship. And the question of Jerusalem is one that's crucial to all vocational enquiry: Is this moment—perhaps unexpected, quite likely unwelcome, possibly incomprehensible—to be my Calvary, these days or weeks my Passiontide, this crisis or illness or conflict my Holy Week—the place where I lose my life to embody the gospel that my life is a gift from God, yielded in baptism for resurrection in the Spirit, made to be a blessing to church and world, a context in which conventional happiness or length of days are of secondary relevance? Anyone who wants to be Jesus's follower must expect such a moment: the Gospels teach disciples to regard lives that encounter such moments as not the exception, but the norm. Of course Nazareth, Galilee, and Jerusalem aren't the only options. Attention also dwells upon the alternatives. Among these, three stand out. The first is Bethlehem. Bethlehem is the place of danger wherein it serves no purpose to stay. There is, for now, no glory in remaining in a place where violence is pressing, friends are few, and conflict is everywhere. Jesus had Golgotha ahead of him; but his parents discerned this was not the moment. Attention asks the question, "What good is being served by you undergoing this danger, threat, and hostility right now?" The second place that demands a question is Egypt. Joseph and Mary were in Egypt for a season. It was a suitable place of escape. But there came a time to return to the Holy Land. Places of escape are appropriate in many lives, timely in particular crises; but attention asks, Have you been too long in Egypt? Has escape become your natural habitat? So aware of your need to run away from danger, have you lost sight of your vocation altogether? The third place that invites enquiry is the upper room—the place where the disciples retreated after the Ascension and before Pentecost. This is the place where fear has kept a light under a bushel, has inclined the slave to bury the talent in the ground—the moment when a person is apparently content with discipleship and resistant to that calling issuing in ministry and/or mission. It may transpire that, as with the disciples, something transformative had to happen—in their case the descent of tongues of fire. But it may equally turn out that the habits of inhibition have corroded the channels of grace.

In many traditions worship ends with words of dismissal such as, "Go in peace to love and serve the Lord." In other words, go and do the thing that only you can do, the thing that God put you here to do. Await no second instruction. Very few people ever receive the level of encouragement they need to be the person that only they can be. The discernment of vocation is about being able to tell a story about the past that includes not only the positive experiences but the negative ones too, and being able perhaps for the first time to perceive how God can use all these experiences for something that would not have been possible to imagine without them. But even then, vocation is seldom a well-trodden path; it is frequently a surprising discovery, and one that needs considerable encouragement and permission. Attention listens to a story, probes a little into where hope and hurt and promise and fear seem to lie, and then ponders, "I wonder what this person really needs to help them 'love and serve the Lord.' " Invariably the person has the answer in their heart, but could not imagine that anyone else would understand, tolerate, or ever endorse that answer. Very occasionally that answer may be disturbing. But much more often the answer is too timid, and attention invites the person's imagination to run even further, to envisage more of what God has in store for them. What attention more often says is, "God is bigger than you think, and you are a bigger part of what God has in mind than you currently imagine."

One of the most fertile scriptural narratives for paying attention to vocation is the departure of Elijah in 2 Kings 2:1–14. It begins with the human reality of how hard it can be to let go. Sometimes one person, or maybe both, hold the hug so long it's clear they have no real strength to release the embrace, where maybe tears, maybe platitudes, maybe silence expresses that there is really nothing to say. It's hard to say whether it's tougher to be the one leaving or the one left behind. The one leaving is heading into the unknown; the one left behind is returning to the known, but without the person who makes the known make sense. Elijah had opened heaven to earth, and that's why he was known as a prophet—one of the greatest. And now Elisha is facing the question, "Where is the Lord, the God of Elijah?"

Deprived, by the presence of the company of the prophets, of the privacy of an intimate farewell, Elisha beholds his master disappear in a whirlwind, and he tears his clothes in two pieces. Since he doesn't have many clothes, that's no small gesture. But Elisha isn't just facing the loss of Elijah. He's facing the inheritance. These are big shoes to fill. Elijah offers a double share of his spirit and his mantle, physically and metaphorically.

The early church identified with this farewell. Like Elijah, Jesus promises there'll be a double portion of his Spirit to come on his disciples after he's gone, and at Pentecost, as at Elijah's departure, there's a lot of wind involved. It's easy to see that this story helped the early Christians perceive Jesus's death and resurrection as standing in this same tradition. For the early disciples the implication of this story must have been clear. It was not for them to mourn Jesus and rend their garments: it was for them to take up the mantle and do what he had done, parting the waters of death and living in the power of the double portion of his Spirit.

And a great deal of being with one another in discernment today takes on the shape of this story. Because much of what it means to be called is to realize it's time to take up the mantle. There's much that makes taking up the mantle challenging. Most people can identify with the sense of being reluctant to say goodbye to Elijah. The world and the church seem so much more secure if we have a father figure, a parent who'll take care of everything, a mentor we can always turn to for advice or recall as an example, or who simply gives a reassuring sense that everything's going to be fine. In one community there was a training event with a crowd of youth workers. The trainer began by saying, "Can we all agree on some ground rules around confidentiality?" The youth workers all laughed; the trainer was offended and confused. But the youth workers explained, "People always start training events like that; but when everyone leaves they gossip like no one had said it. You have to take responsibility for what you share and with whom you share it." What they were saying was, sorry, don't go looking for Elijah; he's gone off in his chariot. You have to create your own safe space now. It was a harsh moment for facing up to an uncomfortable truth.

Another thing that holds many back from taking up the mantle is feeling overwhelmed by the whirlwind. Life brings unexpected, often unwelcome, sometimes sudden events— which can seem like a whirlwind: afterwards it can be hard to recall events in the right order; it transpires there are whole passages of life like national news or wider family events that have completely passed a person by; it feels like nothing will ever be the same again. Both Elisha and the early Christians knew the pain, confusion, denial, and grief of realizing Elijah was gone. And both Elisha and the early Christians knew what it meant to emerge from the whirlwind. And for both Elisha and the early Christians that was the time for them to take up the mantle.

Paying attention to a fellow disciple and being with them means waiting, listening, pondering, and then finally choosing the right moment to say, "I don't care if you're eight or eighty-eight; I don't care if you're new to faith or long in the tooth; I don't care how much you miss Elijah or how scary the whirlwind is. God's calling you. God's sending upon you a double portion of Elijah's spirit. It's time to inherit that mantle. It's your time."

Mystery, as so often, exposes the difference between the convenient and the congruent, the effective and the effervescent, the plausible and the inescapable. While the impatient urge of problem fixing casts its quandaries into an unknown future, the cherishing eye of mystery looks back into the past. If you're called to be a teacher, says the eye of mystery, the chances are you've long been a teacher, long been one who took delight in walking with others as they learned new tricks, made new discoveries, remembered past insights, found confidence to articulate fast-held convictions, implemented ways of enfleshing deeply buried hopes. If you're called to be a priest, senses the ear of mystery, the likelihood is you've long been alert to opportunities to bring reconciliation between the human heart and the heart of God, or between the alienated and the aggrieved; and you've long been seen as a person who embodied grace, inspired hope, triggered faith. The Holy Spirit does bestow gifts upon the called; but more often the Holy Spirit reawakens neglected or underappreciated skills, reinvigorates significant but forgotten dispositions, blesses and fertilizes regretted and buried experiences. Mystery knows that calling is less a career than the renunciation of a career; that it's seldom wisely entered by those who have perfect assurance of what they are doing; that by definition it can only be pursued by disciples who pray daily to be clothed with power from on high; and yet it's a service that brings perfect freedom.

More broadly, mystery assumes one of the fundamental convictions of being with: that setback and hardship, aside from simply being disappointing and sometimes distressing, are the richest source of insight into God and the ways of God. Mystery probes setback and apparent disaster, and says, What is this saying about the vocation you are being drawn toward? And this is where mystery coalesces with **delight**: for delight sees the abundance and not the deficit, reincorporating back into the story items previously seen as distractions, delays, or dissonances. For delight, the key counsel is, Strive to be what only you can be. There's no point in trying in vain to be a pale imitation of somebody else—someone with a different vocation and different ingredients from which the Holy Spirit might concoct a meal. Instead, a person's future, particularly its creative and unique elements, is largely discovered in the process of finding, cherishing, healing, and reintegrating neglected or disowned dimensions of the person's past. Joy is found when for the first time a sad memory becomes a resource for wisdom or an experience to sustain oneself or another through a lean season. Fulfillment comes when the frustration of having an apparently useless gift or the guilt at feeling drawn to a seemingly irrelevant or unhelpful hobby is transcended in that gift or hobby dovetailing within an aspect of ministry or mission. What appeared to be a distracting impulse is now a recognized, affirmed, and welcomed, indeed needed, gift.

This is a characteristic outcome of the ministry of being with because such ministry assumes abundance: it expects to find that the Holy Spirit has given God's people everything they need to worship, befriend, and follow, and thus perceives that the experience of scarcity is more likely to be due to the church's willful or indolent neglect of what's been given than the lack of sufficient generosity or provision in the giver. Meanwhile, being with always assumes that the gifts God has given to the community far exceed the gifts God has given to oneself: ministry and mission are not primarily about developing one's own gifts so as to be all-sufficient but more about identifying, encouraging, and fostering gifts in others so that all may find a blessing.

Mystery, delight, and partnership come together when

discerning how a calling may relate to a job, career, or profession. Mystery listens to the deep yearnings of the soul, the profound, often purposeless joys of the things that a person does for fun, for the individual's own sake, for no reason other than the pleasure to be found in them—the places where a person finds fulfillment, simplicity, peace. Delight pursues particular skills—skills that the person himself or herself may not take particular pride in, but that an observer regards with admiration, relish, even envy. The delight evoked in another may help a person truly value such things, if not as a source of joy in themselves, at least as a blessing to others or to a community; it may also help a person integrate such skills into a sense of vocation by helping chart a way to find a place in a larger story, be painted onto a larger canvas, turn from eccentricities into priceless assets. Partnership brings a pragmatic dimension to the discernment by assessing what passions and skills can actually earn a wage, offer a lifetime or season of work, finance a household, resource a church, pay taxes, support others. Somewhere within this triangle of passion, skill, and income lies the transition from calling to employment.

Turning to **enjoyment** we discover why this chapter isn't titled "being with the normal," or "being with people at every stage of life." The reason is that what people have in common is that they all have the same shepherd: there isn't any such thing as "normal"; from baptism onwards, what distinguishes people is their calling. To enjoy people is to immerse yourself in their particularity, in the details of where they're coming from and the wonder of where they're going, in what makes them unique and special and precious in God's sight. It's to share in the way God beholds them. God made them this way because God wanted one like them: and God wanted one like them because God had a part for them to play in the story that only they could play. To enjoy people is to attend to them while they discover the part they are to play in the story.

Enjoyment describes the way one helps a person move from discipleship into ministry and/or mission. Discipleship says, "I need to learn to be with God and I need to make my way toward being with myself. If I'm not at peace with God and myself, I have no foundation for living." Enjoyment says, "Yes, but you need to learn to see others as a gift and not a threat. Don't you see that my enjoying you, besides affirming, cherishing, and challenging you, enriches and blesses me? That's what ministry and mission do—they're about enjoying the church and the world the way I am enjoying you right now." Enjoyment gently says, "There's so much, so deep, so undiscovered, so rich, so limitless, so joyful in you. You were made for more than this." Enjoyment goes on, "Think about the joy you find in creation—in the delight of a kitten, in the wonder of a rainbow, in the arc of a leaping porpoise, the waft of a skimming pelican, the shimmer of a setting sun, the clip of a chill winter morning, the smash of a breaking wave. Of course creation requires care, work, wariness, expertise, craft, study: but doesn't it give more than it gets? How much more so the church and the world, the theatres for ministry and mission: they demand as much as, if not more than, being with creation; but they too give back more than they take. You've got to give them a chance. And look—here are all the gifts in you that seem to be surplus, far more than you need simply to be a disciple; are you going to bury them in the ground, or leave them lying around like an unwanted Christmas present? And it isn't a passive choice: if you neglect these gifts, they'll eat away at you, they'll turn sour, and, if not used for good, will rot your purpose, skew your vision, eat away at your soul. Enjoy your gifts by applying them to ministry and mission, or they will chew you up from within."

This may seem a more assertive kind of enjoyment than we have expressed elsewhere, but it underlines the point that enjoyment is a teleological practice: it models the life of the

End, the purpose of creation, the fulfillment of the kingdom. If you're not putting your gifts to work, you're not enjoying yourself. If others are not exploring, enhancing, and helping you discover and deepen your gifts, they're not enjoying you. God's enjoyment of us isn't a static thing: it's a dynamic power, in which the Spirit enlivens us, gives us energy, joy, and vigor, and offers us good work to do. That work may change in the course of our life: but it runs from childhood to dotage, and enjoying one other means being with one other as we discover how our gifts are precisely what God is calling for at such a time as this.

Which brings us to **glory**. In many settings at the celebration of the Eucharist, at the moment when the word crosses over into the sacrament, offerings of bread, wine, and money, and sometimes other things, are brought forward and placed upon the altar or table, before the priest or pastor prays the great thanksgiving. This is a depiction of glory: gifts have been given; the congregation has turned those gifts into offerings—the bread of honest toil, the wine of celebration, the money for the furtherance of ministry and mission—and those offerings are now to find their fulfillment in being taken into God's story, from creation to the last day, crystallized in the death and resurrection of Christ, itself embodied in the taking, blessing, breaking, and sharing of the bread and wine as a being united with Christ's body and blood. This is glory because it is humanity and the creation meeting their destiny in companionship with God. It also depicts what glory means for being with the called.

One priest in a challenging neighborhood got a knock at the door one late summer's afternoon from a half-dozen teenage boys. They were holding a shoebox. Inside was a blackbird that they had found near the church, with a damaged wing and a crooked leg. They brought the bird to the priest. It wasn't exactly Galilee, with the people bringing the poor, the blind, and the lame, but in a community where a lot of people had thrown stones at the church it was quite a moment. The priest realized all he was being asked to do was to touch and stroke the bird, to affirm those boys in their compassion. Eventually they all went to the vet together. But the most important thing was to receive that bird as a gift brought forward in an unwitting offertory procession, for the priest to turn that offering into a prayer.

Another time in the same parish a stranger came to the door on a Friday and said he was sending a CD to a record label and wondered if the priest could pray with him as he did so. It was the priest's day off, but it was an impossible request not to honor. They went into the prayer room at the church and the priest held up the CD as if it were the Eucharistic host at the consecration. Four days later the musician knocked at the door and brought the priest four small coins to say thank you. Those coins were a kind of widow's mite: they showed the priest how much that prayer and that touch of his precious CD had meant. It remained one of the priest's most treasured moments in ministry. It was a glimpse of glory.

Glory is, by nature, something that belongs to God. That human beings can perceive it, behold it, enter it, enjoy it, limited and flawed as we are, is a gift of constant wonder known as grace. Being with the called is the daily reflection upon and inhabiting of that grace; constant cherishing of, and invitation to others to share in, the amazing sharing in God's habitation and dwelling—the experience of glory. And that's to be done not by claiming an entitlement or earning a reward, not by demanding justice or achieving a goal, but by gratefully, eagerly, and joyfully employing the gifts one has been given in the story one has been cast in. The parable of the talents becomes the daily psalm of being with the called: "These are not the gifts you asked for or the circumstances you imagined; the cards in your hand were not dealt by you, the other players in the game are not the ones you guessed they would be; but given this context, given your story, given, most of all, God's story, and given the way you've been made, how are you going to enjoy the what, the who, and the where that lie before you? This is how things are: but how are you being called to respond? Which way lies the glory?"

CHAPTER 7

Being with the Troubled

I understand the troubled to be those who are in a predicament significantly of their own making. In this chapter I compare and contrast two narrative accounts of being with the troubled, and try to discern what makes the one more successful than the other—thereby to discover what it means to be with the troubled.

In chapter 16 of George Eliot's novel *Adam Bede* we find an elegant portrayal of a sensitive pastoral conversation.[1] Adolphus Irwine is the Rector of Broxton: a generous, thoughtful man, he lives with his mother and sisters in the rectory. He ministers to the whole community. His former pupil is Arthur Donnithorne, twenty years old, son of the local squire, enlisted in the army and anticipating taking a seat in Parliament. Arthur has an issue weighing heavily on his mind. He has recently developed a passion for, and entered a liaison with, Hetty Sorrel, a local farmworker and orphan, whose beauty is such as to "turn the heads not only of men, but of all intelligent mammals, even of women." The liaison seems set only to ruin

---

1. George Eliot, *Adam Bede* (Oxford: Oxford University Press, 2008), chapter 16.

Hetty and jeopardize Arthur's considerable prospects. Arthur is more mindful of the latter likelihood than the former. Imperfect as his motives may be, Arthur knows he needs to confide in trusted Mr. Irwine. He decides to join the rector for breakfast. The progress of civilization, Eliot sagely observes, makes breakfast the most suitable time for sharing confidences: "mortal sin," it turns out, "is not incompatible with an appetite for muffins." What follows is an exquisite study in what it means to be with, and yet not fully be with, a person who is troubled.

Mr. Irwine is delighted to see his visitor. "Why, this is like old days, Arthur; you haven't been to breakfast with me these five years," he says: but he doesn't raise the eyebrow further about Arthur's unexpected appearance. On entering the breakfast room, Arthur's resolution wavers. "The confidence which he had thought quite easy before, suddenly appeared the most difficult thing in the world to him, and at the very moment of shaking hands he saw his purpose in quite a new light." The prospect of acknowledging his own weakness, misuse of power, and selfishness is, all of a sudden, too humiliating: "Irwine would think him a shilly-shally fellow ever after." Crucially, Mr. Irwine fails to enquire in any detail why Arthur has come.

The conversation meanders on until Mr. Irwine, with ironic prescience, says, "My mother and I have a little discussion about you sometimes: she says, 'I'll never risk a single prophecy on Arthur until I see the woman he falls in love with.'" Mr. Irwine then enjoins Arthur not to let him down and prove old Mrs. Irwine right. Arthur winces and shrinks from telling Mr. Irwine his story: "the mere fact that he was in the presence of an intimate friend, who had not the slightest notion that he had had any such serious internal struggle as he came to confide, rather shook his own belief in the seriousness of the struggle."

Arthur pursues the subject hypothetically. He maintains, "It is hardly an argument against a man's general strength of character that he should be apt to be mastered by love." Mr. Irwine counters, "A man can never do anything at variance with his own nature. He carries within him the germ of his most exceptional action; and if we wise people make eminent fools of ourselves on any particular occasion, we must endure the legitimate conclusion that we carry a few grains of folly to our ounce of wisdom." Mr. Irwine is slow to perceive that Arthur may have a pressing reason for pursuing the argument; but finally he gets there. "He really suspected," Eliot notes, "that Arthur wanted to tell him something, and thought of smoothing the way for him by [a] direct question." But it's too late: Arthur senses there's too much at stake, and he may later come to regret his confession. Mr. Irwine suddenly wonders if Hetty (whom he knows) is occupying Arthur's thoughts; but he dismisses the notion. He realizes Arthur's inclination to change the subject. Eliot slams the door: "The opportunity was gone. While Arthur was hesitating, the rope to which he might have clung had drifted away—he must trust now to his own swimming."

Arthur Donnithorne is, for sure, headstrong, arrogant, selfish, and proud. But he is also anxious, trepidatious, and corrigible. Mr. Irwine gets so much right. Yet in the end the pastoral conversation is a failure. The consequences for Arthur are grim, and for Hetty, catastrophic. What can we learn from this about the practice of being with the troubled?

Mr. Irwine is certainly **present** to Arthur. The Church of England, then and now, makes great play of having resident clergy, available to their parishioners and sharing the warp and weft of community life. Mr. Irwine knows Arthur well. Even his mother has the measure of the young man. They share a meal; as Eliot observes, "One can say everything best over a meal." This is a perfectly orchestrated, indeed highly socially privileged form of presence. One could say all the efforts of those who crafted the condition of the church in nation and locality had come to fruition in making possible a conversation like this. This is a moment for Zacchaeus to announce a change of heart, Levi to set his tax booth aside.

One could perhaps say that Mr. Irwine proceeds to **delight** too rapidly, without passing through the necessary dimensions of **attention** and **mystery**. Mr. Irwine is fond of Arthur—perhaps too fond, such that he fails to take seriously how easily Arthur can feel captivated by the beautiful Hetty, taking advantage of her while telling himself it is all but a passing fancy. Mr. Irwine is thrilled to be joined at breakfast, his moment of male solitude in a largely female household, by another man, in this case a young man whose attention makes the senior man feel less old. He relishes the conversation, not least for the opportunity it gives him to display his sagacity and argumentative flair. There is much delight here.

But there is not enough attention and mystery. Mr. Irwine is sharp. But he doesn't immediately ask Arthur why he's come. Attention always wonders. Mr. Irwine, at this moment, does not. By the time it occurs to Mr. Irwine that something serious might be afoot, a lot has been said, not least by Mr. Irwine himself, that might make a disclosure from Arthur problematic. Mr. Irwine has cast doubt on Arthur's judgment in matters of the heart, has held forth on the significance of character, and has spoken of those who fall into temptation as objects of pity. The fairway is no longer clear for confession. Suddenly an idea dawns on Mr. Irwine—an idea that should have struck him long before. "But I never knew you so inclined for moral discussion, Arthur? Is it some danger of your own that you are considering in this philosophical, general way?" Now Mr. Irwine is all attention. Eliot says, "In asking this question, Mr. Irwine pushed his plate away, threw himself back in his chair, and looked straight at Arthur." But it's too late. With everything that's been said, Arthur can't present his relationship with Hetty as an idle affectation. Mr. Irwine has already made it clear that something of this kind reveals a profound moral flaw. To speak now would be, for Arthur, humiliating. Even so, a direct question could have elicited the truth. But here Mr. Irwine fails in his apprehension of mystery. Too quickly he closes off the myriad possibilities of intrigue and circumstance. Quickly Mr. Irwine thinks of several reasons why no such liaison could have come to pass: Arthur would never see Hetty except at church, he would soon join his regiment, he cared too much about keeping the good opinion of his neighbors. There's not enough mischief, playfulness, or imagination in Mr. Irwine to perceive the truth. And so, fatally, politeness intervenes where direct enquiry was so desperately required: Mr. Irwine, says Eliot, "was too delicate to imply even a friendly curiosity." Disaster ensues.

The encounter discloses the occasional tension between **participation** (the essence of being with) and **partnership** (which is closer to working with). Mr. Irwine is having a good time; he appreciates Arthur's company: he's having a "good day at the office" with excellent company and matters of substance to discuss. But in the process he loses perspective on his own role: he becomes a philosopher rather than a pastor, a duelist in argument rather than a shepherd of souls. Partnership means both parties playing their respective roles so together they can achieve something they could not have aspired to apart. Arthur arrives fully expecting to play his role. But Mr. Irwine is not thoroughly in role—his own need for conversation, his interest in the argument, his desire to win it, and delicate politeness all hold him back from the part he needs to play. It's clear he has the insight: but, as Eliot beautifully crafts the scene, he's overplayed his hand by the time he senses there could be something serious afoot, and his desire for all to be well outweighs his awareness that all might not be. Mr. Irwine's fundamental mistake is that he assumes from beginning to end that Arthur has come to see *him*. But Arthur has come to face the truth about his behavior, his feelings, and his predicament—and Mr. Irwine is important only insofar as he can help Arthur do so. Arthur leaves having not done so—indeed, having dug further into a place of denial and shame and self-deception. Mr. Irwine has been significantly worse than useless, albeit in an agreeable and gentlemanly way. The key to being with is **enjoyment**. Mr. Irwine enjoys himself: but he does not fully "enjoy" Arthur. If he was enjoying Arthur, and the pastoral conversation that is under way, he would gladly entertain all possible outcomes, all likely motivations, all fanciful dimensions, all undisclosed eventualities. Instead, he narrows down the range of possibility to that which sets him in a good light, enables him to retain an avuncular wisdom, and keeps Arthur from having to announce what he fully intended to reveal. Harsh as it might sound, fundamentally Mr. Irwine is using Arthur rather than enjoying him. Arthur is of course using Mr. Irwine, but that's not the point. Mr. Irwine is a pastor. All his energies should be focused on enjoying moments such as this. It is a devastating failure. Because there is no enjoyment, there is no **glory**.

A humbler, and considerably more tortured, but nonetheless more positive account of being with the troubled is found in Hannah Kent's novel *Burial Rites*.[2] A servant, Agnes Magnusdottir, stands condemned of inciting a neighbor to murder two men, including her master and lover, Natan. There are no prisons in Iceland in the 1820s, so Agnes is kept over the winter with a family at a local farm, awaiting execu-

2. Hannah Kent, *Burial Rites* (London: Picador, 2013). Page references are given in the text.

138

tion. A Lutheran priest, Thorvardur Jónsson, known as Tóti, is assigned to visit her and prepare her for her death. Over the bleak months of waiting he makes several visits to the farmstead and abides with her as she begins to articulate her story and her fears. Tóti initially shrinks from the task: "he caught himself wishing that he were ill, gravely ill" to give him an excuse not to ride to see her for the first time (30). He wonders whether he should be "kind and welcoming, or stern and impenetrable." He mouths the word "murderess" to himself over and again. But as he nears the farm, he whispers, "I will save her" (32). But he fluffs his opening encounter with Agnes, fails to elicit a word from her, and retreats, clumsily and too hastily. Chastising himself later for his cowardice, he nonetheless perceives many features of her appearance: along with the "sharp pungency of a neglected body," "leprous colours" resembling "a new corpse," a ripe, yellow bruise on her chin. He enters a church and prays, "Strengthen my ability to withstand the sight of suffering, so that I might do Your work in relieving those who endure it." And he asks God to guard his heart "against the *horror* this woman inspires in me" (50, italics original). Before his next visit he asks his father, also a priest, "What would you say to her?" His father answers, impatiently, "Who says you'll need to say anything?" (75).

Tóti's second interview with Agnes goes worse than the first. He stumbles over formal, rehearsed language and she quickly realizes she's dealing with a fumbling "red-headed boy" who has no more idea how to face this journey than she does. She chose him to be her confessor because he once, several years before, assisted her across a river. He, it transpires, has forgotten (78–84). Again, Tóti feels like reneging on his commitment to prepare her for death. But, he reflects, "perhaps she didn't have a friend left in the world" (88). So he keeps visiting, and gradually listening begins to replace prepared words, trust starts to develop, and Agnes, without either party realizing it, teaches Tóti how to be with her. He discovers that truth looks different for her, an abandoned child, with no place to lay her head—and the truth has not set her free. Now she starts to tell him of her deep anger, her experience that men cannot cope with an intelligent woman. For the first time she says, "I'm glad you're here" (133). For the first time she allows him to pray for her in her fear. His gentle questioning, while she knits and remembers, elicits more and more of her story. Tóti can hardly breathe as she tells it (150).

When Tóti is asked to give an account of his ministry to the district commissioner, he discloses that religious rebuke has not proved a profitable course of action. Instead of the stern threat of brimstone, he has found "the gentle enquiring tones of a friend" best suited to "draw the curtain to her soul" (166). The commissioner is unimpressed, regarding Agnes as "reticent, secretive, and guilty" (172).

Agnes shares with Tóti a dream she once had in which she was walking barefoot across snow, and felt she would die from fear. A young man appeared, wearing a priest's collar, and, though she was still terrified, he gave her his hand, and it was a comfort. Then the ground gave way, she fell into the darkness, and the ground closed over her again (184). Tóti realizes he is that priest. From this time on, even though their winter conversations, being necessarily indoors, were overheard by the rest of the household, Agnes begins finally to speak of her relationship with Natan, and "it was as though she could not stop talking, even if she wanted to" (212).

Tóti becomes ill with fever, and his father, probably rightly, suspects that the fever has been brought on by becoming emotionally overengaged with Agnes's plight and her story. But eventually Tóti returns to the farm to tell Agnes that her execution has been set for six days later, and to promise that he will be there with her (317). And he is, standing right beside her, holding her hand as she approaches the scaffold, ignoring the smell emanating from the loose bowel of her fear. Finally he says, squeezing her hand, "I won't let go of you. God is all around us, Agnes. I won't ever let go." Then the ax falls.

What does Tóti get right that Mr. Irwine gets wrong? Of course he has a ministry of **presence**, with his regular visits to the farm in which Agnes serves out her time before execution. He withstands his own fears and failures and tentativeness and keeps visiting until the membrane between him and Agnes begins to thin. Unlike Mr. Irwine, who assumes all is well with Arthur, Tóti is under no illusions he's facing a challenging conversation, which means his **attention** is all the sharper. Several times he observes precise details about Agnes, of appearance and demeanor, such that he begins to be able to read her before she begins to be able to trust him with her words. Tóti has no great pastoral skill at putting people at their ease or making small talk. But Agnes, after the testy opening exchanges, never doubts his profound attention. They both know what they are about, and charm and social ease become irrelevant.

The crucial transition comes when he realizes that his carefully rehearsed words are proving counterproductive. Gentle enquiry is a better way of demonstrating God's concern for her; close observation guides the enquiry. This is the territory of **mystery** and **delight**. Only when he's able to lay aside the narrow task of hearing her confession of sin, and prepared to offer as long as it takes to discover the truth of her story, does she stop seeming the caged monster of everyone's imagination and start becoming a person of depth, texture, struggle, and humility: a person evidently more sinned against than sinning. Openness to **mystery** and **delight** can yield danger: the narrative hints of moments of sexual attraction, rooted in the visceral context of the story told and the threats pending. While mindful of this dimension, Tóti's actions remain both public and exemplary: the inevitably brief timeframe of the relationship provides both a stimulus to intimacy and a protection against anything beyond conversation and reassuring touch. But Tóti's conviction that there are hidden depths to Agnes beyond her notoriety is crucial to her eventually being embraced by her host family and finding a sense of belonging she had never before known.

The practice of **participation** is largely conducted by the host family, initially hostile, long suspicious, but eventually, through respect born of hard, shared labor in daunting Icelandic conditions, accepting and embracing. Yet there is participation too in the early exchanges between Agnes and Tóti, where neither hides the fact that the situation has been thrust upon them both, and neither knows how to proceed. The key to **partnership** in this story is that Tóti finds the ability to relax his role, at least in its formal dimensions, despite criticism from his father and from the district commissioner. He's embarrassed on one occasion when his father points out that he's left his New Testament behind as he's leaving the house to go to the farm. Certain boundaries remain—Agnes continues to address him as Reverend, for example. But he learns that simply reprimanding Agnes of her sin and awaiting repentance is useless. First she must be given space to discover for herself what has happened and why—only then does the distinction between what she has done and what she has suffered begin to apply. Tóti's role is to give her the space to make that discovery and, through remembering, probing, cherishing, but not judging, to help her construct a truthful story.

Unlike Mr. Irwine, who enjoys himself but finally uses Arthur, Tóti truly **enjoys** Agnes. That, in many ways, is what the novel is about: everyone in Agnes's life hitherto has used her, from her father who seduced a servant woman to that same woman, her mother, who abandoned her at age six and on in a sad procession until Natan who manipulated and took advantage of her in a netherworld between housemistress and simply mistress. Tóti is the first person who enjoys her, not as a means to an end, but as an end in herself. Initially he comes to the farm to use her—to extract from her a confession to secure for her the grace of God. But gradually he learns what it means truly to enjoy her, with all the attention and mystery and delight that involves. And because there is true enjoyment, there is **glory**. Agnes is not saved from the ax. But she's saved from the misery of a world of deceit, bullying, cruelty, suspicion, envy, and violence, and finds, in her final weeks, a world of truth, honesty, integrity, kindness, trust, and gentleness. It's too much to say hope, or even faith: but she's been transformed from a feral, fearful creature into a dignified, articulate woman, and is in the process of becoming fully alive at the point she is executed. In such unpropitious circumstances, this is indeed glory.

Ideally, being with the troubled involves enabling the speaker to locate his or her story in some poignant way within the scriptural story. It may be in wilderness or exile; in passion or in the upper room; on the Sea of Galilee in a storm or with Jonah in the belly of the whale. Sometimes, as with Agnes's situation, given her skepticism about the church and its ministers, it can be hard to find an invitation to do this. But the listener, unlike Mr. Irwine, should always be alert for an opportunity.

Besides this role of renarration, there are, in summary, three things Tóti does that Mr. Irwine doesn't do—three things that are crucial to being with the troubled. The first is to stay with the formless and void, to hover over the deep, until it becomes creation, until the speaker finds words and weaves together silences—to show the speaker that the painful things she says cause the listener to wince, that the terrible things she's done grieve but don't shock, that the miserable things she's experienced sadden the listener, and that the unresolved situation she's in doesn't make the listener rush in with a solution to fix it or a rapid remedy to settle it or a joke or a story to distract from or belittle it.

The second thing is, when the speaker has reached the end of her story, to demonstrate and check understanding by inviting her to explore further and explain more fully. Like an osteopath or a chiropractor passing a gentle hand over a patient's back, this is about stroking in one place and pushing in another, trying to find the tender area and see which movements make it worse and better. It involves remarks like, "I wonder which was your lowest moment in this whole saga," or, "I wonder what it's like to realize you don't come from a happy family," or, "Do you still dream about what happened?" What this is trying to do is to give permission to say the scariest, most embarrassing, shameful, or bitterly painful thing and then show that it's possible to live beyond it, outside it, around it, and then begin to face it down together and make a story that's not poisoned or dominated by it.

The final thing in being with the troubled is to say, "Is that the whole story?" Of course it never is. It's important to stay silent for a while, to indicate it's okay to say more. That silence is the crucial moment in the whole conversation. It's a moment of lingering, a stretching out of the hands and dwelling over the sensitive place—a moment like the way, during a Eucharist, priests hold out their arms over the bread and wine when asking the Holy Spirit to infuse these earthly elements with heavenly grace. It's an invitation to the speaker to go deeper, to go right down to the bottom of the pond if that's where the mystery lies and the pain resides. It's a promise in which, like Tóti at Agnes's execution, the listener is saying "I'll be here as you go way down there."

Tóti is clumsy, faltering, emotionally fragile, and liturgically inarticulate. Mr. Irwine is urbane, wise, and generous. But when it comes to being with the troubled, only one of them has got a clue.

CHAPTER 8

Being with the Hurt

A t the outset of this chapter I need to distinguish its theme from that of the previous one and the subsequent ones. Being hurt means being in a trying, distressing, and sometimes painful season—but one that should, one hopes, sooner or later come to an end. For the hurt, damage may well remain, but forgiveness will, all being well, eventually come; for the afflicted, whose suffering will be considered in the next chapter, symptoms may last a long while, but healing is, in time, expected. In that respect being hurt or sick differs from being challenged or dying. The challenged (and their caregivers) and the dying are coping with or facing the prospect of a permanent condition or end, something that isn't going to "get better." It's a qualitative difference, not a quantitative one. There are overlaps, and, at times—for example, in the case of severe injury or illness—it may not be clear which is in question; but the two situations are essentially different. One is about patience, endurance, and grace, given that God will eventually bring about the needed change. The other is about faith, hope, and courage, given the reality and finality of an ending.

This chapter on hurt and the one on affliction are also

different from the account of being with the troubled. The troubled are those who, to a greater or lesser degree, have brought their burdens on themselves—through ignorance, weakness, or their own deliberate fault—and are trying to find the humility, grace, hope, and courage to face the reality of what they've done, the perplexing choices that confront them, and the daunting prospect of restoring dignity and integrity. By contrast, the hurt and the afflicted are those who, for the most part, are facing trials they've done little or nothing to bring about. The troubled are coming to terms with the power they have and the damage they've proved capable of doing with it. The hurt and the sick are apprehending their own powerlessness and seeking to discover how to function despite it.

And so to hurt. Being with the hurt is centrally about recognizing without reservation the pain, grief, and anger of suffering that's been inflicted by a third party, unconsciously, casually, negligently, or deliberately; waiting patiently until recipients of such wounds begin to renarrate their reality as a story in which they can see beyond their own powerlessness and the perpetrator's guilt; and being a companion as victims start to articulate a world, however unsought and no doubt still bearing scars of damage, that would not have been imaginable without the incident that brought so much sadness. The word for this process is "peace."

Though untrue, it's widely believed that Berwick-upon-Tweed, the most northerly town in England, was, until recently, at war with Russia. Because Berwick over the centuries had so frequently passed between Scottish and English possession, there was a period in the eighteenth century when official treaties specifically named the town. The town was not named in the peace accords that ended the Crimean War in 1856. Hence the rumor that Berwick and Russia remained at war. When the London correspondent of *Pravda*, the official newspaper of the Communist Party of the Soviet Union, visited the town in 1966, the mayor proclaimed, with benign dignity, "Please tell the Russian people that they can sleep peacefully in their beds."

If only all conflict could be dispelled by the discovery of a historical misunderstanding and the bland reassurances of a provincial dignitary. The reality is that conflict is endemic in the human condition. To be with the hurt means to believe that peace is not a past state to which we expect, and feel entitled, to return, but is instead an aspiration toward which we invite God to lead us and at which we never expect fully to arrive. This requires an account of the nature of peace and the nature of God. It also means facing the reality of violence and the question of whether that violence is so damaging to the Christian faith as to discredit it altogether. But finally an awareness and recognition of the historic legacy and contemporary reality of violence can support the hurt in their quest for peace.

For the writer of Ephesians, peace is Jesus. This is, to use a word found several times in Ephesians, a **mystery**. "He is our peace," says the letter (Eph. 2:14), because in his body he breaks down the enmity between God and humanity and between different parts of humanity, one with another. In God the Father, Christians see the creative animating dynamism of all things, the power that not only brings things to life but orders them so they relate to one another as pattern and beauty and plenty rather than as conflict and deficit and diminishment. In God the Son, Christians see that God is fundamentally relationship, not only with humanity but also within the godhead itself, that God's will to make and restore relationship is limitless and costly—indeed, it's the heart of everything, the essence of creation and salvation. In God the Holy Spirit, Christians see God's meticulous, constant, and relentless will to bring to fruition all that was embodied in Christ, however long it takes, however much resistance is met, however tortuous the process. In the Holy Trinity, Christians see the nature of God in the interaction of these three persons; not competing, not envious, not in tension, but complementary, overflowing, gracious: so harmonious that we call them three, so melodious that we call them one. It's this notion of the Holy Trinity that Christians believe Ephesians invokes when it says of Jesus, "He is our peace."

This account contrasts with other influential notions of peace. It points out the *dynamism* of the Trinity, thus highlighting the contrast with a portrayal of peace as static, fixed, and uneventful. Peace can't be captured by a painting, or by an emblem such as a dove carrying a twig, or a rainbow. One of the problems of a static, anodyne account of peace is that it's nothing like as interesting as violence. The dynamic account of peace points out the *narrative* of God's creating all things, and entering into relationship with creation, definitively in Jesus, and bearing with humanity through the Holy Spirit. Thus it emphasizes that peace is always part of a narrative. It doesn't just appear between the clouds, like a breaking sun, and it doesn't just arrive from the sky, like a descending meteor. It's not like a ball that you lost and are looking for in the long grass, and it's not like the name of a school friend you rack your brains to remember when homecoming weekend approaches. It's more like the flourishing of a relationship—something you probably aren't aware of when you're in the midst of it, but nonetheless makes life worth living and brings you your greatest joy. It affirms that making and restoring relationship is in the *nature* of God, and thus asserts that peace isn't simply an occasional and short-term tactic that God adopts to resolve periodic disputes. On the contrary, there's no moment when God isn't engaged in a process of peace, whether by the Father's intricate weaving of one creature beside another, the Son's coming and living and dying and rising that God's relationship with us be embodied and restored, or the Spirit's painstaking re-presentation of the Son's work in every generation. Peace isn't an attribute or an approach; it's inherent and integral.

It notes that the work of the Holy Spirit is *patient* and tortuous, thus seeking to dispel sentimental versions of peace that bypass the tooth-and-claw bloodiness of ecology and the elongated processes of rectifying wrongs. Peace isn't easy, isn't simple, and isn't often in any degree fully realized. But that's no reason not to seek it with all your heart. It affirms that God is *Trinity*, in other words is always three-in-one and one-in-three, thus underlining that joy and identity don't lie in detached, autonomous independence, but in the constant to-and-fro of mutual interdependence. Peace isn't the still waters of a lake in the mountains far away from strife; it's always contingent upon other people, one's own fragility, and the configurations of tentative harmony conjured up by the connections between the two. Salvation is not about immunity from the world's viruses. It doesn't mean becoming free-standing individuals impervious to change, chance, or challenge. It means being in the throng of a dance, where every mistake is turned into something creative and hopeful, every misunderstanding leads to deeper wisdom, and every regret becomes a source of insight and renewal.

Thus peace is not a past state to which we expect, and feel entitled, to return, but is instead an aspiration toward which we invite God to lead us and at which we never expect fully to arrive. Peace is a process, not an original starting point or a foreseeable destination. It's about relationships. Relationships are not like buildings, which are opened when all is working well and begin to decay from that moment on. They're more like gardens, which begin from the dust, and gradually take root and flourish, and yet need pruning and attention and are never in a place of static perfection or repose. Sometimes toward the end of a conflict people refer to the "peace process"; but in truth the phrase is a tautology, because peace is always a process.

Peace requires **partnership**. It's a process, and it can't, finally, be done by one party alone. When the Bourbon dynasty returned to power in France in 1815, twenty-two years after the execution of Louis XVI at the guillotine, and named the new king Louis XVIII, thus asserting the validity of Louis XVI's uncrowned son, it was said the Bourbons had learned nothing and forgotten nothing. In other words, no process of peace had been undergone and the political settlement was superficial. It lasted no more than fifteen years. After the Treaty of Versailles in 1919, Marshal Foch, head of the French forces in the First World War, said, "This is not a peace. It is an armistice for twenty years." He was only out by sixty-five days. Again there was not a thorough process of peace. There was simply a settlement.

What does a process of peace involve? We can talk in broad terms about the following steps.

1. The parties involved need to be able to see beyond the conflict, to have a sense of their respective identities as not inherently wrapped up in being at fundamental enmity with one another. They need to begin to imagine a future bigger than the past.
2. There needs to be an acknowledgment of a condition of enmity, recognition that this is not the best intention of either party, and thus cessation of active hostility, whether by ceasefire, third-party intervention, or outright surrender.
3. There has to be some attempt to tell a truthful story that acknowledges resentments and bitterness but also shortcomings and bad faith on both sides.

4. At this stage or later there needs to be some form of apology, that is to say a form of words that expresses both acknowledgment of responsibility, without resort to mitigating excuse, and genuine sorrow, not simply for the significant hurt and the irreplaceable damage but also for the wrong intention that brought about such hurt and damage.

5. There should be some kind of penance, that's to say nonverbal and substantial recompense, not only for the intangible hurt and pain, but also for the tangible damage and loss.

6. There may be a written or similarly understood agreement about how things will be from now on, endeavoring to avert the circumstances and discourage the behaviors that gave rise to the conflict.

We may call these the minimal conditions of the process—ones that don't explicitly require theological narration. The maximal conditions, which do, almost inevitably, involve theological narration, include

7. Repentance. Repentance is somewhat like the moment in a twelve-step recovery program where one admits that one has lost control of one's life, that the hatred has become unmanageable, and that one has become powerless to stop the conflict on one's own. In other words, repentance is an admission that an apology, which suggests an out-of-character misstep, is not enough, because the truth is that one is addicted to conflict and violence. It's a recognition that, without God's help, one's own sustained resolution, and a supportive community, there's no hope of breaking the cycle of dependence.

8. This may helpfully issue in confession. Confession will ideally include not just recognition of culpability and

genuine remorse but an exhaustive articulation of specific acts of wrongdoing.

9. The maximal conditions refer most prominently to forgiveness. In this sense forgiveness is a decision by one or more parties not to be defined by resentment or antagonism, to seek a bigger life than one constantly overshadowed by this painful story, and to allow one's perception of the harm received no longer to stand in highlighted isolation but to blend slowly into the myriad of wrongs and griefs to which the world has been subject across time.

10. Then there's reconciliation. Reconciliation means seeing a future in active relationship with the one who has perpetrated so much harm; not to sustain life by keeping out of the other's way or erecting impenetrable fences, but to believe and discover that the former enemy has part of the key to one's own flourishing and that without that key one will remain in some sense still in the prison of hatred. Ideally, reconciliation means turning an enemy into an ally, perhaps even a friend.

11. And then comes healing. Genuine healing means finding oneself in a place where one can say, "I am a wiser, deeper, better person than I would have been had all this not happened. I still bear the scars, but, like Jesus's scars on Easter Day, those wounds are an indication of glory, a sign of love, and an emblem of peace." This is a moment of paradoxical **delight**. Healing is an anticipation of

12. Resurrection. Resurrection is, finally, the goal of salvation and the end of a peace process. And in naming the goal of salvation and of a peace process as resurrection, we disclose that salvation and a peace process are ultimately the same thing. Salvation is a peace process. A peace process is the seeking of salvation. And here's the crucial point. Our engagement in a peace process and God's saving res-

urrection of Jesus are different in degree but not in kind. Engaging in the process of peace is the fundamental way we imitate the saving work of God in Christ. Thus it is a glimpse of **glory.**

This is a twelve-step process: seeing an identity beyond enmity, ceasefire, telling a truthful story, apology, penance, interim agreement, repentance, confession, forgiveness, reconciliation, healing, and resurrection. It sometimes takes decades. It doesn't always happen in this strict order. But laying it out like this as a process makes it clear how a bland call for healing in the face of a gunman's massacre or a profound betrayal is invariably a facile platitude that misses the extent and depth of the process involved to get there. You can't just jump in at stage nine without taking account of the previous eight stages. If vital elements are rushed or left out, the process is likely to be delayed or stalled rather than advanced. A limb badly set has to be broken again to be healed.

People often ponder whether it's helpful or appropriate to say "sorry" in the face of historic injustices such as slavery or colonialism. The answer should be clear from the twelve-stage process I've just laid out: if "sorry" is something like stage four in a process where it's a recognition of the irreversibility of the previous three stages and is a declaration of commitment to the subsequent seven stages, then yes, it's helpful and appropriate to say "sorry." But on its own, without such a recognition and such a commitment, then "sorry" may well be, and will likely be experienced as, superficial, self-serving, manipulative, and inadequate. Jennifer Harvey evoked a good deal of comment when, in her book *Dear White Christians,* she encouraged white Christians to leave aside the self-serving language of reconciliation and take up instead the more challenging disciplines of reparation, including repentance and confession.[1] It's not an either/or. What Jennifer Harvey is rightly doing is highlighting that repentance and conversion and penance must precede the talk of reconciliation; and that without them, reconciliation is an idle tale.

In October 2006 Marie Roberts wrote the following words to her Amish neighbors in Lancaster County, Pennsylvania: "Your love for our family has helped to provide the healing we so desperately need. Gifts you've given have touched our hearts in a way no words can describe. Your compassion has reached beyond our family, beyond our community, and is changing our world, and for this we sincerely thank you." A few days earlier Marie's husband Charles had shot ten girls aged six to thirteen in a one-room schoolhouse in West Nickel Mines in the nearby Amish Bart Township. No one was pretending that after such a horrifying slaughter a process of peace could take place overnight. In any case the suicide of the killer made a full reconciliation impossible. But within hours some key elements of a process were in place: the wounded, the bereaved, and the family of the perpetrator were all able to see identities beyond the roles of enmity; retribution was immediately ruled out; a wider context, such as the depression of the perpetrator, was envisaged; face-to-face meeting, and solidarity in the wake of grief, was under way.

The alternatives to peace are broadly the same as the alternatives to God. There are, from the Christian perspective, two. The first is fantasy. Fantasy, when it becomes an all-pervading attitude to life, is another word for idolatry. The replacement of God by a god of our own making, be that reason, nature, culture, nation, sport, art, the self, the state, society, desire, or personal relationships, is known as idolatry. What's less frequently pointed out is that the intoxication of vio-

1. Jennifer Harvey, *Dear White Christians: For Those Still Longing for Racial Reconciliation* (Grand Rapids: Eerdmans, 2014).

lence—the drug-like phantasm that seeks in violent means a route to benevolent ends, that fixates on short-term success at the expense of long-term erosion of authority, legitimacy, patience, and trust—is a similar kind of fantasy. It's a fantasy that supposes all opposition, resistance, disagreement, obstacle, and subversion can be overcome through degrees of obliteration, or the threat of them.

The second alternative to peace is oblivion. Oblivion means the deliberate removal of oneself from conscious, rational, relational, quotidian human existence. When a gunman massacres a crowd and then turns the weapon on himself, he's doing two different things. The massacre of the crowd is an act of fantasy, a grotesque game in which he's transfixed by the destructive power of his weapon and his effect on those around him. But the turning of the weapon on himself is an act of oblivion—a statement that living with the result of his actions is intolerable. The difference between fantasy and oblivion is that in fantasy, the participant is unaware that he is living a lie—a lie that may be shared by many others and whose falsity may not come to light for a long time; whereas by seeking oblivion, the agent is deliberately searching out an alternative to the boredom, discomfort, or horror of current existence. Fantasy is a fruit of hope, albeit false hope; oblivion is the result of despair, albeit false despair.

Violence is, from the Christian perspective, either fantasy or oblivion. It represents the fantasy of a solution to things that can seldom be solved, or oblivion from things that are too daunting to see for what they are. Those who advocate for limited use of violence to do good, usually to promote justice and secure a more lasting future peace, invariably claim that those who disdain the use of violence are living a fantasy. The advocates' fantasy is to believe violence is something they can control. An alcoholic discovers that first you drink it, then it drinks you. The same is true of violence. Violence enslaves those who believe they can master it, uses those who presume they can make it their tool. When Jesus said, "Those who live by the sword, die by the sword," he didn't mean it's always the case that they die in battle; he meant that once you give your life to the sword, the sword owns you (see Matt. 26:52). Like any addiction, the moment you decide to walk away from it, you find you've entered a world where all the exit doors are locked. But there's another way in which the use of violence is a fantasy. Just as life is suffused with God, if only we are willing to recognize it, so life is a constant process of making peace—interrupted, complicated, disrupted, and delayed by episodes of violence. It's the violence, rather than the peace, that represents the insurgence of fantasy, the indulgence of distraction, the parenthesis of oblivion from the deeper, longer, harder work of peace. Blessed are the peacemakers; for they reflect to a fitful world the abiding nature of God.

Violence is an insurgency. Violence refers to the attempt to take advantage of an imbalance of force by the threat or infliction of physical, sexual, psychological, or emotional injury by one or more people on one or more others. It's the reversion from what society sees as legitimate uses of forms of imbalance such as sporting success or economic advantage based on greater fitness, skill, and strength, to nonlegitimate uses, such as enslavement by physical constraint or abuse by practices of domination. It can include state-sanctioned violence, where usually nonlegitimate physical actions are commanded for a limited period to restore order or achieve a greater good; collective violence, where a group of people acting outside the law intimidate or exploit others; and personal attack, where an individual is subject to the momentary or sustained physical imposition of power resulting in short- or long-term harm. It's the ultimate form of ill-use rather than blessed **enjoyment**.

Given such a broad definition, it goes without saying that we live in a world where violence is widespread and always has been. Societies that pride themselves on being civilized are founded on the rule of law. Under the rule of law a strict distinction is made between state-sanctioned violence and the other kinds, and victims of the other kinds may have every expectation that such attacks are the exception and that their assailants will be brought to account. Such societies, even though the incidence of violence may be relatively low and the rule of law may largely prevail, only deserve the designation peaceful if significant numbers of people are actively engaged in processes like the ones I've been describing. Without such processes in place, mechanisms of intervention, arrest, trial, and incarceration or warning, deployment, combat, and victory are not peace, but rather the construction of fragile armistices in which people have learned nothing and forgotten nothing.

In one of the prophecies frequently understood by Christians as fulfilled in Christ, Isaiah describes the child born unto us as the "Prince of Peace" (Isa. 9:6). If Christ has come, and is the Prince of Peace, violence seems to pose three challenges to Christianity. They are weighty questions, and they strike at the heart of Christianity's philosophical and moral authority. To respond to them requires profound and unswerving **attention**.

The first question is, if Christ has brought peace, why is there still so much violence? Christians believe Jesus didn't just expose the world's realities and model a better way; he changed those fundamental realities and inaugurated a new possibility. So it's bewildering when signs of that change are hard to identify, or visible, but obscured by signs of the opposite. The conventional answers are that God's will is not imposed, but offered—that people are free to say no; and that the transformation of cross and resurrection is a down payment of a gift that will be fully realized at the end of time. An answer closer to a reflection on the nature of God would argue that, in the sending of the Spirit, the Father and the Son have given the church a process by which to perceive and broker peace.

But that answer just invites the second question: If Christianity is committed to peace, why has it not healed the virus of violence? Have Jesus in his human and divine nature and the church in the power of the Spirit proved a failure? It's common to quote words widely attributed to the cultural anthropologist Margaret Mead, "Never doubt that a small group of thoughtful, committed citizens can change the world; indeed, it's the only thing that ever has." But rather more often even such worthy citizens fail in their mission. The world doesn't fundamentally change. Ignorance, perversity, and folly still stalk the land with relative impunity. Violence may be a sign of the prevalence of sin and evil; but it may just as easily be an indication that sin and evil are under pressure and are resorting to desperate means to gain the ascendancy. Either way, Christianity is not committed to a presumption of progress. The twelve disciples had maximal exposure to Jesus, yet collapsed under the strain of the Passion. The church has generally followed suit. However closely Christianity is enfolded in peace, it's not a solution to violence.

And so to the most troubling of the three questions to a contemporary conscience: How do we account for the extent of the violence that has been precipitated, perpetrated, or exacerbated by Christians, both toward others and among themselves? Where does the fault lie? Again the conventional answer is that the fault lies in ourselves: sin lurketh at the door, as much for his successors as for Cain himself. The envy, pride, insecurity, ignorance, perversity, and folly of Cain is reproduced in untold circumstances, and Abel and his successors' blood continues to cry from the ground.

But the horrifying legacy and present reality of Christians inflicting violence on others and one another is too profound an affront simply to be explained by blaming individuals for their sin. The difference between sin and evil is that sin is committed by those who know that what they are doing is wrong. By contrast, evil engulfs individuals and groups and persuades them that this hideous action they are pursuing is in fact right and just and true. Many, perhaps most Christians who have perpetrated violence on others and one another haven't recognized that they've let themselves and the church down; they've assumed they were upholding the faith in what they were doing. It's too simple to call this sin. This is the perversion of the faith, dressed up as righteousness. It's what the church calls heresy.

Of course there've been occasions when Christians in their relations with others and one another have fallen short of the virtues to which they are called and to which they themselves aspire. Christianity is all about the redemption of the fallen and the forgiveness of sins. But that's not the issue here. The issue is false doctrine and its embodiment in grotesque distortions of Christian ethics, people regarding as worthy and upright what is in fact shameful and cruel, treating neighbors that should be enjoyed as threats to be exterminated, strangers that should be cherished as dangers that must be banished, those whose different faith should challenge and enrich one's own as infidels that must be expunged from the face of the earth. It's a fundamental failure of **participation** in and with the ways of God.

There's a gray area in the middle, between the sins Christians know are wrong and are embarrassed to acknowledge, and the evil that engulfs Christians and induces them to designate as good what is in fact very bad. That gray area concerns what's often called justice, and it involves upholding, asserting, or restoring the ground rules of civilized existence in the face of chaos and the breakdown of law and order. What constitutes reasonable force in arresting an armed fugitive, calming a riot, or separating warring parties? Here the words of one contemporary theologian offer helpful guidance. He believes being a Christian means not keeping a consistent ethical stance or adhering to a set of rules, but looking for opportunities actively to share a gracious privilege. Christians, he says, "guide their lives not so much by 'How can I avoid doing wrong?' or even 'How can I do the right?' as by 'How can I be a reconciling presence in the life of my neighbor?' From this perspective," he maintains, "I might justify firm nonviolent restraint, but certainly never killing."[2] Being with is disclosed as the way to peace. The path begins with **presence**.

Killing doesn't reconcile. It puts a person in a place from which they cannot be reconciled. It puts them outside what at the beginning of my remarks I called "the process." It nowhere figures among the twelve-stage process I set out at the beginning of the chapter. It's true that you can't have a peace process without a minimum level of safeguarded order. That's why this gray area is so hard to adjudicate. But that helps us see the force of the claim that being a Christian is less about being in the right or being an arbitrator of the legal and much more about looking for opportunities actively to share a gracious privilege. As Paul found in prison, and Christ found on the *via dolorosa*, you can find yourself oppressed, and you can be in a place where the rule of law is damaged or absent—but you can still be active in sharing that gracious privilege. That's what presence means in the face of conflict.

And that's the Christian response to the most alarming of the possible inferences from the egregious violent errors

---

2. John Howard Yoder, *What Would You Do?* 2nd ed. (Scottdale, PA: Herald, 1992), 40.

of the faithful through the centuries. We've seen that it's not enough to talk about sinful individuals—we must instead acknowledge a mistaken gospel, a virus of evil displacing what should be untold good. But deeper even than that is a fear that the prevalence of violence across the centuries discloses not just a mistaken gospel, but a flawed God. Is God impotent in the face of evil, or is God somehow complicit? Is a faith founded on an act of violence—namely the crucifixion, prefigured by God's call upon Abraham to sacrifice his son Isaac and the Hebrews' slaughter of the Passover lambs—inextricably bound up in violence from beginning to end? It's a serious charge.

To respond to it Christians need to steer a careful course that embraces Christ's humanity as well as his divinity. A pious ethic that assumes God is all things mild and reasonable ignores the Jesus who brought not peace but a sword, spoke of turning son against father and casting fire upon earth, hurled money-changers from the Temple, assumed his disciples would be tortured by the authorities, and called on his followers to take up their crosses.[3] But none of this sacralizes or embraces violence. Christians assume the crucifixion of Jesus is the last sacrifice, the end of violence, the last, most desperate, and most abject failure of the attempt to subvert the process and destroy the peace of God. Henceforth all violence is a denial of what has been demonstrated and established in the crucifixion; all violence will be redeemed by resurrection, whether in this existence in the form of forgiveness and healing, or in another existence in the form of everlasting life with God. Violence has already lost; to employ it is to salute a defeated king, to consume a discredited medication, to invest in a bankrupt company, to deal in a fake cur-

3. See Terry Eagleton, *Culture and the Death of God* (New Haven and London: Yale University Press, 2014), 136.

rency. The heresy of violence can be turned to good; all things can: but it can never be turned into *a* good. Peace isn't just a plausible technique: it's the nature of God. To set oneself outside it is to line up on the wrong side of eternity.

What we have seen is that being with the hurt cannot take place simply in isolation from the great scars of wrong that pervade the world. Christians have a word for the process by which they see beyond conflict and find an identity not immersed in enmity; by which violence is recognized, acknowledged, and named; by which the sin through which Christians fall short is distinguished from the evil by which they have been engulfed; by which wounded parties seek to tell a truthful story, make penance, and try to establish an agreement that articulates the wisdom needed to prevent a resumption of embattlement; by which they enter into repentance, forgiveness, reconciliation, healing, and resurrection. The word for that process is "church."

When Christians say the church is the body of Christ, they mean that Christ is the embodiment of that process; Christ's incarnation means that Christians can always know that that process is at the heart of God. The limbs of Christ's body are there to bring about reconciliation: that is their raison d'être. As Ephesians (2:14-16) puts it, referring to Jews and gentiles, "in his flesh he has made both groups into one and has broken down the dividing wall, that is, the hostility between us"; moreover his purpose thereby is to "reconcile both groups to God in one body through the cross." In other words the purpose of Jesus's incarnation and crucifixion is for Jews and gentiles to be with God and one another. To say that the church has often fallen short of its calling to be an agent of reconciliation between Christians and others and among Christians themselves is no casual recognition: it's an acknowledgment of the extent to which the church has denied itself, betrayed its identity—failed, in short, to be church.

The Bible is the story of this process carried out between God and human beings. It's the story of God repeatedly being defined beyond enmity, perceiving Israel beyond enmity, and inviting Israel to understand itself beyond enmity, and of God offering a record of wisdom gained, telling a truthful story, reaching out in forgiveness and reconciliation and healing and resurrection. There is no Bible that's not, from beginning to end, the story of this peace process. Violence challenges, insults, undermines, delays, and damages this process; but it never derails it. The violence of the cross is the ultimate challenge but proves to be the consummate vindication of the process, because there the violence is inflicted on the second person of the Trinity, and thus becomes an attack on peace itself. The light shone in the darkness, and the darkness did not finally overcome it (John 1:5).

This becomes the foundation of all evangelism, because evangelism is nothing more or less than inviting people to join the process—or, to use a term we considered earlier, looking for opportunities to share a gracious privilege. Evangelism means saying, "Do you want to join the process?"—which is a more focused way of saying, "Do you long for peace?" Peter comes to Jesus and says, "Lord, if another member of the church sins against me, how often should I forgive? As many as seven times?"—and Jesus replies, "Not seven times, but, I tell you, seventy-seven times" (Matt. 18:21-22). If evangelism is inviting people to join the process, then saying "you must forgive seventy-seven times" is saying, there isn't any alternative to the peace process. The only other options are, on the one hand, the fantasy or oblivion of violence, or on the other hand, the diversion to other, more agreeable and achievable peace processes besides the one you unfortunately find yourself intractably in the middle of. The injunction to forgive seventy-seven times is saying, wherever you look, there's a process of peace—in some cases needed and not begun, in other cases foundering, in other cases making headway, in other cases again showing green shoots of healing resurrection. And in the end, all delay, distraction, or diversion in relation to joining a process of peace is providing fertile soil for, perhaps colluding with, and at worst fostering violence.

All evangelism is a call not just for the transformation of the stranger but for the renewal of the church. If the church is calling the stranger to join the process, the church must constantly be engaged in that process itself. And here's the crucial point: this process isn't a time-consuming, specialized, and demanding distraction or prologue to the ministry, practice, life, and mission of the church. It is the ministry, practice, life, and mission of the church. Neither is it a necessary preparation for entering the fellowship and presence of God. It is the nature of God. It's the way we experience salvation, which is simply the point where our lives and God's life intersect. An important way in which the church's understanding of evangelism has grown in recent times lies in its understanding of the violence of relationship between humankind and the earth, sea, and skies, and the need for a process of reconciliation there. It's a complicated form of reconciliation, because it's not reciprocal in the same way that a process between people usually is. But the basic shape of evangelism—inviting people into a larger, richer, truer life and out of the impoverishment of estrangement and enmity—remains the same.

This notion of peace as a process also becomes a touchstone for all questions of ethics. In 1 Corinthians Paul discusses different practices in worship, including speaking in tongues. He doesn't rule particular practices in or out, but suggests all should be ordered as to what builds up the church. What builds up the church becomes a touchstone for all ministry and fellowship. The process of peace, understood as Ephesians describes it, and in particular what advances or facilitates that process, offers a similarly promising touchstone for mission. In this sense otherwise very humble actions that build trust and understanding, record wisdom gained from conflict, or express sorrow, regret, or apology may be described as peacemaking, since they advance or facilitate the process of making peace. Missionaries are those who engage in one or more of the stages of the process, intentionally recognizing their partnership with and dependence on those who engage in the other stages.

One character known to many in Durham, North Carolina, was the late Ann Atwater. Ann was a domestic help who was transformed by community organizing into a 1960s civil rights leader. In striving to enhance the educational and economic opportunities of her children, Ann found herself shoulder to shoulder with an unlikely comrade: C. P. Ellis, a leading local member of the Ku Klux Klan. At a crucial moment, while grudgingly arranging a public meeting around education, Ann and C. P. gradually realized what they had in common was much more profound and much more urgent than what divided them. Their peaceable action of building institutions, raising aspirations, and organizing communities—but also of listening, sharing humility, and changing their minds—was an unglamorous, unstylish, undramatic process of peace.

It is to such as these that the kingdom of heaven belongs. For salvation isn't, in the end, being rescued from a fiery furnace and delivered up to an ethereal cloud. Salvation is being redirected from a spiral of fantasy and oblivion to a gracious, ordered, liberating, and often sequential process of reconciliation and healing. The problem with violence is not that it's something real that we should keep a secret; the problem is that it's either fantasy or oblivion, an illusion of our power and a false assertion of our control. The final discovery about truth and peace and salvation is that ultimately they're the same thing.

Being with the Hurt

I have structured this chapter differently from the others because I believe that the violence that brings about hurt has a character different from the other conditions I've been exploring. It has a compelling, almost viral hold on the imagination, and only detailed theological renarration can inscribe a different story. Without that different story it is hard to avoid a cycle of retaliation and retribution. Thus in this context the practices of being with presuppose formation in this alternative story—which is why I have taken the whole chapter to outline what that story is and how it differs from the conventional one. Because to be with the hurt means to trust that that story is true.

CHAPTER 9

Being with the Afflicted

Affliction is the state where one experiences a profound degree of pain and suffering in a condition one does not anticipate to be permanent, but where one's distress cannot be identified as the result of being a wayward individual, but only as an impersonal disease or unfortunate setback.

Being with the afflicted, as will be clear from the explorations of the previous chapter, is not primarily about facilitating as rapid and agreeable as possible a resumption of life in the daily capabilities and attitudes that had preceded the injury or illness. It's about accompanying a person through a process. The aspiration is not to fix a problem but to enter a mystery. It's for the person not simply to "get better" or "get over it" but more richly to enter into an experience of God's kingdom. It's not for a person to be able to resume previous life and "forget all about it"; nothing, say it gently, will be quite the same again: yet the hope is that this new reality will be truer, wiser, and deeper than the previous one.

Such ministry begins, as ever, with **presence**. Presence—being close, showing up, not being deterred or scared away, making a journey to see with one's own eyes, not flinching from the new reality—is the first way to appreciate what's happened and what's happening. Something has changed—there's been news, a diagnosis, the announcement of a course of treatment—any or all of which feels like a diminishment, a loss, a disruption at least and a distressing or disastrous development at worst. Presence means taking time to let it sink in, dwell on its unique features, begin to witness the bifurcation of the story that would have been without it (for all its unknowns) and what seems, at least initially, to be the smaller and more impoverished story that ensues from it. Just as it takes a while from the moment when a blow is received to the time a bruise appears, so presence registers that there's a difference between knowing something's happened and discerning its scope and ramifications.

Likewise presence is essentially—but not necessarily—wordless. Presence says, "I don't know what this is, what this means, how deep this goes, how damaging this may be; it could all be over tomorrow, it may last a lifetime; it might keep getting worse, it may go in phases, it may be bad at the start and then alleviate. I have no idea. But I'm here whichever course it takes, and my companionship doesn't depend on which course it takes. In the unknown and dismay and distress of this sickness, some things can be relied upon. If you need to, you can start building from there." And presence goes on saying such things, however long, however opaque, and however inconsistent the setback is. Being with begins with presence, because presence embodies the fundamental disposition to say, "This isn't about me. I probably have no wisdom or experience to bring to it. I don't predicate my engagement on seeing signs of positive change. I am willing to accept this may not turn out to be a happy story. I am empty-handed."

As presence yields **attention**, the general becomes the particular. Not to be abandoned is foundational. But in time, details are everything. This sickness matters because it's like the one a parent had, it's similar in pattern or timing to a momentous previous experience, it's affecting precisely the limb or organ that's crucial for work or play. This injury is poignant because it undermines the thing most longed for, the relationship most vulnerable, the characteristic most doubted. Being with and paying attention to the afflicted isn't about having sage advice or a quasi-medical remedy. It's about remembering precise connections, perceiving significant developments, recognizing grievous setbacks.

Attention is all about making subtle distinctions. Sickness can involve agonizing loss; it can also trigger tremendous pain. It can bring about considerable discomfort and provoke considerable disruption and inconvenience. These are all distressing: but they are not the same. Paying close attention, and being able to remember and play back such distinctions to a person, with tenderness, can aid perspective and help a narrative or trajectory of events to emerge. In the face of a blanket of anger, or an overwhelming sense of powerlessness, it can offer texture and nuance and maneuverability, from which a person can begin to perceive priorities and find footholds.

Attention discloses **mystery**. Mystery is the point where one begins to broaden one's identity from that of victim to that of learner, discoverer, even adventurer. When one passes from the kingdom of the well to the kingdom of the sick, one sees things from a new perspective. In the words of Susan Sontag, "Illness is the night-side of life, a more onerous citizenship. Everyone who is born holds dual citizenship, in the kingdom of the well and in the kingdom of the sick. Although we all prefer to use only the good passport, sooner or later each of us is obliged, at least for a spell, to identify ourselves as citizens of that other place."[1]

---

1. Susan Sontag, *Illness as Metaphor* (New York: Farrar, Straus & Giroux, 1998), 3.

What can one see from the kingdom of the sick? And how can one be with a person—now acknowledged as a stranger—from that foreign kingdom? One dimension is to dwell in a land beyond blame. The intensity of anger leads almost inevitably to blame. It arises from powerlessness and a sense of injustice, and it trails unstoppably toward a person or cause on which to focus the fury. But mystery resists the impulse to follow the logic of distress–anger–attribution of culpability–vengeance–satisfaction, or even distress–diagnosis–treatment–cure. Mystery looks beyond blame, and beyond cause, and recognizes the fragility, transience, contingency, and fragility of things, and yet their meaning-laden, fertile, and allusive nature. Before hastening to resolve the situation, still less making it as tidy as possible, mystery abides in the shadows of the unique, the unexpected, the incomprehensible, and the unimaginable, suspecting that real life dwells there. The doors to such places surround the kingdom of the sick.

Those who dwell in the kingdom of the sick, or, we might say, the commonwealth of the wounded and broken, make another discovery. If access to the unimaginable and incomprehensible is an avenue into depth, then there's also an avenue into breadth: and that is the recognition of those whose company one now keeps. This can be a very contemporary unveiling of support groups, blogsites, clinical research cohorts, or solidarity movements that focus experience and expertise on those with similar struggles. But mystery is more about an imaginative entering into a shadowy netherworld and finding there a new ability to empathize with those whose lives have not gone to plan, have been subject to catastrophe, distress, or disaster. The isolation of sickness can be matched by the companionship of new comrades.

Mystery, once it has set aside the reflex to solve and fix, can explore the resonances between healing and forgiving.

Initially they may seem poles apart: the one is an unconscious process of recovery after random invasion of illness without obvious cause, the other is a conscious act of will in the face of deliberate harm wrought by an identifiable third party. Mystery discloses inflections to this apparent distance. One is that healing is seldom simply about the alleviation or disappearance of symptoms, but usually involves acceptance, learning, deeper wisdom, understanding, greater compassion, extended empathy, new perspective. Another is that, even when the origin or source of the sickness is inanimate, anger and hatred toward it can be as intense as when the perpetrator is a known individual; and some kind of process of making peace, at least analogous to forgiveness, is probably required for healing to take root. However much we might like to keep soulless sickness and passionate hurt separate, they have many things in common and can inform one another extensively and creatively.

It may seem absurd to talk, in the face of sickness, of **delight**. Delight isn't saying "Hey—it's great to have this illness!" It's seeing the person beyond the condition. Mystery means moving from the default mode of solution-finding and problem-solving. Those in the kingdom of the sick are invariably surrounded by well-meaning advice and counsel from people who assume, without question, that the task is to return, as quickly and effortlessly as possible, to the kingdom of the well, and that help and support mean, primarily, pointing to the best facilitators or catalysts of that return. This is a classic case of working for displacing being with. Of course there's a place for remedy and cure. But the role of being with is to stay in the present, even if—especially if—there's no return to the kingdom of the well. When people are suffering, they don't just need an alleviation of their tangible condition: they need companionship in the midst of their pain and distress. Seeking or suggesting a solution can often be a way of not seeing the pain or not abiding with the sufferer. Sufferers need to know that their company is still of as much—perhaps more—value if they don't "get better" or "get over it" as if they do. This is the territory of delight.

Taking delight in and with a person who is sick means attending to how much there is about the person that the sickness doesn't diminish—and perhaps enhances. Adversity can bring out admirable qualities in some people. Even when it does not, and despite intense feelings in the immediate aftermath of serious harm or onset of significant illness, it seldom truly "changes everything." Delight rejoices in what doesn't change, in what may be even truer because of this setback, or even more remarkable in spite of it. That may not only be a quality in the person himself or herself, a quality of endurance, courage, grace, gentleness, forbearance, patience, or insight; it may just as much be the sheer goodness of being alive, the gift of each day, the wonder, albeit slow, of forgiveness or healing, the resilience of the human spirit. And it may be a moment of renewal in recentering the person away from himself or herself, to recognize how much of the world—no longer wholly or primarily *his or her* world—goes on unaffected and unaware, beautiful and inspiring, relentless and unceasing, with its own dignity, dynamism, and integrity. This is how what could be an occasion of resentment and bitterness—anger at betrayal, offense, or rejection, frustration at illness or intractable condition—can become an entry point to renewal, a stimulus to faith or a doorway to humility.

Perhaps the most poignant dimension of being with in relation to sickness is **participation**. Participation says, "Only you can experience this, but I will walk alongside you as you do so. This may be an isolating and lonely season, but I'm not going to leave you alone in this. Your life may have altered beyond recognition, but my life is going to be different too. You may change your mood and your attitude to this setback many times, but I'm going to walk at your pace and dwell in your time. You may not have words to express what you're going through: I'm content with silence. You may just need to know someone is there. I can touch you gently and hold your hand in the darkness. You may wonder how long till the dawn. I'm not in a hurry. You may feel you're getting boring. I'm not in this for entertainment. You may worry you're being a burden. I'll look after ensuring I keep engaging with the rest of my life; I won't be helping you if I drop everything in an unsustainable way. You may be ashamed to be showing your fury and weakness and impatience and cowardice. I'm just glad for the gift of your honesty and transparency and trust."

The children's book *Now One Foot, Now the Other* tells the story of Bobby.[2] Bobby's a toddler. He's named after his beloved grandfather, Bob, who lives with Bobby's family. Bobby's favorite game is to pile up all his building blocks, one on top of another, till they rise high into the air. At the very top he always puts the one with an elephant painted on the side. He calls it the elephant block. As Bobby begins to get taller, his grandfather Bob teaches Bobby to walk, patiently standing behind him and saying, "Now one foot, now the other. Now one foot, now the other"—hour after hour. You see young Bobby's body folded into his grandfather's as they walk together.

One day Bob has a stroke. Bobby's lost his best friend. It's a terrible ache and sadness. After a long time Bob returns from the hospital. But Bob's unable to speak or register things spoken to him. Bobby, now about five years old, is determined to restore their relationship. But he gets no response from his grandfather for many weeks. One day Bobby is building the high tower of building blocks while Bob watches vacantly

---

2. Tomie dePaola, *Now One Foot, Now the Other* (London: Puffin, 2006).

from the chair beside him. But then, amazingly but unmistakably, just as he's nearing the very top, Bobby hears his grandfather mumble the words "Elephant ... block." Immediately Bobby knows Bob is going to get better. As the recovery gains pace, young Bobby takes his grandfather outside to learn to walk again. In a glorious reversal of the earlier scene, Bob's body is folded into his grandson's as he relearns to make each tentative step. The story ends with Bobby saying to Bob the very words Bob had once repeated so frequently to his grandson: "Now one foot, now the other." Bobby begins the story being guided by his grandfather and ends by being the one doing the guiding.

This story marks the transition from participation into **partnership**. Partnership recognizes that this new affliction has altered the dynamic of a number of relationships. As in the story of Bob, a person who is used to being the guide may become, for a season, the guided. While partnership comes closer to working with than being with, the crucial thing to remember is that partnership is not about working for. Partnership does not mean turning support into fetching medicines or doing grocery trips or cooking meals or buying thoughtful books or flowers or food. There may be a place for all such things, but the ministry of being with is alert to the way such activity is often an avoidance of staying with the suffering person in silent, powerless, patient recognition of the depth of what she is experiencing. Partnership may be tempted to say, "Let me do that ... why don't I just deal with this ... I can sort it out, don't worry." But the sick person may want or need to do it herself, however inefficiently or clumsily, and however painful or exasperating it may be for a companion to watch. Partnership means having a constant eye on the goal to which both parties are together aiming. "Let me feed you your lunch" may be a tender offer to share in what would normally be a routine activity a person might do for herself. But it could alternatively be a working-for determination to see the goal as dealing with lunch as quickly and efficiently as possible, and a refusal to engage with a larger goal. That larger goal might be patiently sitting beside as a person slowly and perhaps painfully learns to feed herself again: the renewed dignity, and growing confidence, and sense of achievement being more significant than the amount of food transferred and the speed with which it's all done. The person captivated by working for may say, "I'm just trying to be useful." To which the questions are, "Why has this suddenly become about what you need to feel or to do?," "Useful for what?—Why do you presume you are best placed to understand what's most useful?" and, "Maybe the most useful thing you can do is offer silent presence, quiet reassurance, and gentle encouragement."

At its best, partnership names the way a profound breakdown or disappointment, or a serious setback or illness, can create a new community, or renew an existing one. Life can seem more intense, each conversation more significant, every gesture more freighted, resonant, poignant. Acquaintances that seemed dull or peripheral can come into their own as their wisdom, patience, or experience becomes newly helpful or vital. Relationships that had been neglected or strained can be reinvigorated in an infusion of compassion, solidarity, or kindness. For being profoundly hurt or acutely unwell invariably displaces a person from the (admittedly false, but nonetheless widely sought) ideal of the invulnerable individual, for whom relationships are a consumer choice and need is no more than a logistical challenge, and reclothes the person as a tender recipient of others' mercy, support, and sympathy. Vulnerability creates relationship just as much as invulnerability diminishes it. Partnership is about recognizing where walking alongside one another allows reciprocity to develop, such that some things are best done by another person, and allowing them to do such things can deepen a relationship and foster mutual respect and appreciation. When a person is in tears, it's sometimes best to be silent, to hold a hand or offer a hug; but there are moments when one can say, "Would you like me to pray?"; there are times when one can say, "Would you like me to call the nurse?"; there are occasions where one can even say, "This is a tough time, but you've been through even worse than this, and we're going to get through this together; and even if we don't, I'm not going to leave you to face it alone."

Partnership has a particular significance in the case of those who believe their sickness did have some kind of a third-party cause. This is for two reasons. The first concerns the process of reconciliation outlined in the previous chapter. Being with a person who has experienced profound disappointment, betrayal, humiliation, rejection, or heartbreak, when someone else's folly, ignorance, or perversity has been the principal cause, means remaining always aware of some kind of journey toward wholeness. That journey, sooner or later, has to include some kind of engagement with the perpetrator of the damage. Being with a person enduring such distress means being sensitive to when is not the right time, but presuming that, eventually, there will be a right time—and that the journey toward healing has to include steps such as telling a truthful story, forgiving, and being reconciled. Feelings may be too raw, and rushing things is invariably counterproductive; but healing does not ultimately lie in suppression, distraction, and forgetfulness. Being with in partnership means at some stage asking the question, "Is this, perhaps, the right time?"; and if the answer is no, having the courage, at a later date, to ask the question again.

The second significance of partnership in the case of this kind of affliction is a genuine case of working with, bordering on working for. It's the role of an intermediary. A person who's hurt may resist a process of reconciliation because the wound is so deep, the feelings of anger and hatred and horror so sharp that the person almost doesn't know himself. But another reason may be that he genuinely has no idea— or may harbor misgivings—about whether the perpetrator recognizes herself as the cause of damage and is willing to confess, make reparation, and seek forgiveness. To make the first move in the face of such a wall of unknowns is daunting, because it risks exacerbating the wound. Which is why an intermediary can be so helpful: a person who can make initial contact, assess whether the time might be ripe for a meeting, reassure a penitent perpetrator that she will face something more conciliatory than mere fury, and encourage the person who understands himself as the victim to believe there is reason to hope for a process to bear some fruit. Offering to be such an intermediary is a way of being with a person who's been hurt that recognizes both the necessity of eventually contemplating reconciliation and the potential personal cost. Needless to say, the role of the mediator isn't to make judgments, still less to assign blame; it's simply to restore the with.

While the presumption of being with the sick is that this is a season that will come to an end—that healing, at least in significant degree, will ensue—that opening judgment may turn out to be wrong. It may be a sickness unto death; it might be that this is an injury that never heals. This is the moment to recognize that, and move the perception of being with from illness to death, from the afflicted to the dying.

I have left till the end the question of how to pray in the face of sickness, because I want to insist that ministry means being with—and intercessory prayer, in this context, may revert to a form of working for. It's not that working for is wrong—but that it should be firmly grounded in and facilitative of being with. Prayer is, in this case, the territory of enjoyment—in this case almost indistinguishable from the dimension of **glory**. When Jesus hears Lazarus is ill, he says, "This illness does not lead to death; rather it is for God's glory, so that the Son of God may be glorified through it" (John 11:4). Enjoying sickness, like delight, doesn't mean being pleased to experience it or finding happiness in it. It means ceasing simply to see it as an alien, arbitrary, absurd intrusion and seeking to perceive how it might be a gift. A theological lens for perceiving hurt and sickness as gift is transfiguration.

Other forms of prayer are also helpful in the face of sickness. The prayer of incarnation is one that looks for Christ to be present in and beside the supportive companion. It is the archetypal prayer of being with—that through the Holy Spirit, Christ who releases us from the prison of the past through forgiveness and from the fear of the future through everlasting life may enable us to dwell in the present in faith and hope and love. It's always in tension with the prayer of resurrection—the longing to move quickly through the process of truth-telling and wisdom-discerning and get straight to the healing and transformation and tangible hand of the Holy Spirit. As with all intercessory prayer, but in a more intense way, the prayer of resurrection is a request for God to bring forward some of the joys of the Last Day and realize them in this present hour. It seems to be the way it worked in the Gospels and the early church—and there's a lingering suspicion that maybe it's how it works for faithful people today.

In this light the prayer of transfiguration sees genuine purpose—rather than evil or absurdity—in the unsought and unwelcome sickness. It endeavors not to obliterate or work around the distress but to persist *through* it. This is how it's a form of enjoyment—because it seeks not just to use the hurt or sickness by dismantling it, but to enjoy it and see it as a way of becoming closer to God and aligning with God's ways. It appreciates that this is a season of enhanced awareness, heightened sensitivity, greater concentration—and, in this sense, truer living. It differs from the prayer of incarnation in that it looks for God not simply beside the trauma, but in the trauma—a trauma that can provoke empathy with other sufferers or identification with the suffering of Christ. It differs from the prayer of resurrection because it sees this moment of existence as the place of encounter with God, not as a prelude to an encounter that can begin when this setback has been overcome.

The transfiguration account tells us that Jesus "was transfigured before them, and his face shone like the sun, and his clothes became dazzling white" (Matt. 17:2). This immediately follows his first prediction of the passion and the disciples' bewilderment that through suffering could come glory. That bewilderment abides among disciples to this day. Being with the sick means following the logic of Christ's reasoning on the road to Caesarea Philippi, and being willing to stare into both light and darkness and see the face of God.

The transfiguration account portrays the human condition—of ignorance, mortality, and in some cases affliction—as the wearing of a veil. A veil is a temporary barrier. It can either keep something in or prevent something getting out. Every veil assumes a moment of unveiling, and creates suspense and tension until such a moment arises. Sickness can be understood to bring about a veil of this kind.

Michaela Mabinty DePrince was born Mabinty Bangura in Sierra Leone in 1995, in the midst of a civil war. Her father was killed in the conflict and her mother died of starvation. At the age of four she was in the hands of her uncle, who sold her to an orphanage. In addition to her poverty, she suffered discrimination because she had a pigment condition that created spots on her skin that attracted ridicule and ostracism. One day in the orphanage a magazine was blown by the wind into Michaela's hands. On its cover she saw a ballet dancer. Her face looked so happy. Michaela said, "I want to be as happy as her one day." She folded the picture and never let it go. From the orphanage Michaela was taken by a dangerous road across the border to Guinea, from there to Ghana, where she was adopted by an American family and began a whole new life in New Jersey. Through extraordinary dedication and the constant support of her adoptive parents, Michaela fulfilled her dream of becoming a ballet dancer, and today, still only in her early twenties, she's a principal dancer with the Dutch National Ballet.[3]

Michaela's story is a narrative of four kinds of unveiling. The first and most obvious was the unveiling of deprivation. It's hard to imagine anyone facing greater social disadvantage. She was an orphan, she was in utter poverty, she was growing up in the heat of civil war in one of the poorest nations of the world, and she was at the mercy of men who bought and sold her and could take any and every kind of advantage of her. But somehow through a mixture of chance, accident, kindness, and benefaction she escaped her prison and the veil was drawn back.

The second unveiling was the unveiling of apathy. For Michaela, the central moment in her story was the day she saw that magazine picture of the smiling ballet dancer. That kindled in her an ambition, a longing, a dream—and that aspiration led her to strive, to work, to persuade, to study, to practice, to strain every sinew to reach her goal. It turned out she had talent, but that talent would have come to nothing without the sacrifice and dedication that turned it into achievement. She overcame adversity through a burning passion.

The third unveiling was the unveiling of prejudice. Michaela faced prejudice from the very beginning of her life be-

3. Her story is told in Michaela and Elaine DePrince, *Taking Flight: From War Orphan to Star Ballerina* (New York: Alfred A. Knopf, 2014).

cause of the vitiligo skin condition that gave her an unusual appearance. But she faced a more subtle kind of prejudice in the US where it seemed the whole ballet establishment was set against black dancers, regarding their physique as too athletic and not sufficiently artistic. This third veil isn't just the bad luck of being born into terrible circumstances; it's about the prison of social attitudes and racism and discrimination that stifle even a person determined by every means to rise above her disadvantages.

And the fourth unveiling was the unveiling of isolation. It's no use just having determination and dedication if everyone's against you. Orphaned Michaela somehow found friends. Some like her uncle and the orphanage owner were more concerned about themselves than about her; others like her orphaned friend and later adopted sister, and her adopted parents in New Jersey, were like angels of mercy in a world of fear.

Being with the afflicted is about finding ways to remove each of these veils from the inside. Deprivation, apathy, prejudice, and isolation can all be overcome. For the sick, it's invariably such veils that cause more affliction than the illness itself. When deprivation is overcome, apathy healed, prejudice subverted, and isolation dissolved, the afflicted doesn't become a different person; but all the veils come down, and it's like for the first time the person is standing in the light. Christians have a word for this. It's called transfiguration.

The transfiguration is the crossroads moment in the gospel, where Jesus turns from ministry in Galilee to death in Jerusalem, from being a prophet who teaches and heals to being a priest who suffers and dies. The Israelites were taught that God was so holy that anyone who saw God would die. So even though Moses didn't die when he received the Ten Commandments from God on Mount Sinai, he still veiled his face afterwards so the Israelites wouldn't suffer from the sight of his holiness. So, for the Israelites, a veil was a form of protection from being overwhelmed by God. Saint Paul turns that round. He says that that veil prevented the Israelites recognizing Christ until the Holy Spirit took the veil away.

The Holy Spirit takes away the veil of deprivation because Peter, James, and John have no social advantage, not even a home to call their own, but Christ is revealed to them in glory anyway. The Holy Spirit takes away the veil of apathy because even though the disciples had no idea what they were saying or doing and said nothing to anyone afterwards—after the resurrection—they realized they'd seen a prefigurement on the Mount of Transfiguration and here the story is in the Gospel anyway. The Holy Spirit takes away the veil of prejudice because this account comes straight after Jesus has had a fight with Peter, because Peter told him the messiah could not suffer and die, but Jesus said this was God's way of saying, "I will be with you always, whatever happens." The Holy Spirit takes away the veil of isolation because in being surrounded by Elijah and Moses Jesus is surrounded by Israel, and in being accompanied by Peter, James, and John he's surrounded by the church; and so the story's telling us that when we are about God's business we're never alone.

The expression "the scales fell from my eyes" comes from another transfiguration account, creating just as much a hinge of that story when Jesus appears to Paul and Paul turns from oppressor of the church to its greatest advocate. In that case the veil is represented by Paul's blindness. This is what transfiguration does: it dazzles us with the wonder of God, so much that the veil is removed from our eyes, the veil of deprivation, of apathy, of prejudice, and of isolation, and our lives are changed as deeply and wonderfully as Michaela's was from lonely orphan to principal ballerina.

Sickness isn't a veil. But being with the afflicted means

anticipating that when the veil is removed—a veil imposed by circumstance, by another's cruelty, by tired habit, or by the person's own inhibition—the scales will fall from the afflicted person's eyes, and she will see truth, see God, more truly through and because of that affliction than ever before. Even when others, maybe all, have lost sight of the hope, the future, the call, the person being with the afflicted remembers, and, when the moment arises, whispers that, like Michaela, "You were made to dance."

CHAPTER 10

Being with the Challenged

The difference between the challenged and the afflicted is that the former are facing a condition they assume to be permanent, whereas the latter are addressing a circumstance or illness they believe they will overcome. It goes without saying that everyone faces a mixture of challenges and afflictions in their lives; but there's no doubt that some do so in ways that are overwhelming and pervasive, and it is being with such people that is the concern of this chapter.

I refer to four kinds of challenges: (1) those that are permanent, life-altering, but not defining, such as a severe sight impairment that leaves a person heavily dependent on the other four senses, a mobility issue that leaves the five senses intact but presents constant demands and strains, or a stroke that immobilizes one or more limbs or faculties; (2) those that threaten an irreversible decline, such as various kinds of dementia; (3) those that are permanent and profoundly inhibiting in mind and/or body, and in some cases experienced by others as distressing to be around; and (4) those that are like a recurrent sickness, intermittent but debilitating, intractable but not constant, and in some cases open to medication, like depression or some forms of epilepsy. Together these present a broad diversity, as other chapters have done in different ways. Here I seek to offer some common themes that highlight the assumptions and practices of the ministry of being with. But my emphasis is on the second and third scenarios—ones where the person's condition has put her in some significant sense out of reach, apparently unresponsive, mentally not, or no longer, fully there.

In this case the place to begin is with **mystery**. Simply put, the ministry of being with sees extensive disability and profound, irreversible, advancing illness as a mystery and not a problem. It doesn't approach persons facing major physical or mental challenges assuming their deficit, but is committed to perceive their abundance. It doesn't assume that all parties, the persons themselves and all who know them, are working above all for a change in their situation. It doesn't treat them as fundamentally needy, miserable, or pitiable. It doesn't define people by what they're not. It regards their own perception of and language for who and what they are as the template for understandings of their identity.

But avoiding the language of tragedy, curse, and deficit doesn't mean renouncing all sentiments of anger, loss, and lament. Of course there is grief and discouragement. Why does creation come with so many unresolved glitches? Why are those potholes in the road apparently so unevenly distributed? Did Jesus not say he came "that they may have life, and have it abundantly" (John 10:10)? Is this really abundant life, surrounded as it is by so many hardships, challenges, demands, and needs, and limited as it is in diverse ways? These are among the many complaints that, especially when accompanied by pain, evoke tears, frustration, fury, resentment, dismay, struggle, and sometimes despair. But from the perspective of mystery, the lingering temptation that dismantles joy and provokes dissatisfaction is comparison. It's the difference between receiving as grace and demanding as entitlement. It's about the confusion of jealousy and envy.

The difference is subtle, but vital. Jealousy is the anxiety of losing what you rightly have. Envy is the yearning to acquire what you don't have, but somebody else has. We frequently read in scripture that our God is a jealous God. If envy and jealousy were the same thing, that would be an absurd statement. What—God looking at other gods and thinking they do better miracles or came up with a better idea than creation? How ridiculous. But a God who treasures us with that unselfconscious smile of effervescent joy, and doesn't mind who sees and who knows—yes, God is like that. A jealous God is part of the wonder of grace: God doesn't want a hundred other things—God wants us. Nothing else. We're the cream. God's the cat. Our jealous God is smiling from ear to ear.

So God is jealous. But we—we are envious. We just can't be glad for what we have. We are compulsively looking at what others have and feeling impoverished by the comparison. In so doing we objectify the lives of others, seeing them as a series of commodities we could somehow acquire or that we in some way feel entitled to. Meanwhile, we diminish our own lives, seeing only their scarcity, never their plenitude. Witness the parable of the late-hired laborers in Matthew 20:1–15. The early-hired laborers are envious. They don't see why they shouldn't get more—a lot more—than those hired late in the day. Our sympathies are all with them; whether you see them as Israel and gentiles, lifelong believers and deathbed converts, or different kinds of exploited labor in many parts of the world today, the issue seems one of pure justice: if you work hard and long you get rewarded, if you work just as hard and twice as long you get doubly rewarded. Surely.

But what if the agreed "daily wage" is forgiveness and

eternal life? The only response is overflowing gratitude and indescribable joy. God's grace can't be halved or multiplied. It's ridiculous to demand "double eternal life" or "triple forgiveness." There's only one reason why we'd ask for it—nay, demand it—and that's because our envy has so consumed us that we can't enjoy what we have for fear that someone else might have better. For the dismantling of envy, what's required is the rehabilitation of healthy jealousy. To develop a sense of God's grace as precious, we must guard it jealously, nurture it, foster it, seek ways to deepen and enrich it. The time we spend comparing ourselves with others is time wasted.

Jealousy is a teleological sentiment. For on the last day we each shall come face-to-face with God, and we will say, "I took you for an envious God, constantly looking around at others, and so I became an envious person, restlessly comparing and looking to left and right, assuming others had it so good. All the time I was looking here, there, and everywhere, thinking you were the same. But now, standing here before you, seeing your piercing and utterly loving gaze, I understand I was wrong. The truth is, you're a jealous God: all the time, you were just looking at me." Being with the challenged is to practice such gracious jealousy: to say, "I want to practice a grace that is made perfect in weakness. I have no desire for you to turn into someone else. I want you simply to be the best *you* you can be. What could kill you is not your condition but the denial of grace through the contagion of envy. I am here to encourage you in receiving the grace of life, of existence, love, forgiveness, redemption. And to convince you that, whatever happens, you will not be alone."

The significance of **presence** is the easily overlooked but vital recognition that a profound impulse in cultures past and present has been to keep what I've called "the challenged" out of view. For a host of reasons—whether impairment of some kind was regarded as punishment, whether the so-called imperfection was feared as infectious, whether households could not bear the load of a nonproductive member in an agricultural or industrial subsistence economy, or whether the cult of independence and autonomy has made extensive physical or mental challenges seem an intolerable affront to oneself or others—presence is in some circumstances a prophetic act in itself. Presence proclaims value: it says to the person with advanced dementia, "You are still important. You are still my mother, grandfather, fellow member of the body of Christ, neighbor. You still have a great deal to give me. You are still a human being." Presence also says, "I see you. Because you can't always put yourself in front of my eyes, that doesn't mean you are of any less importance. You are not just your past: you are your present, too." In this sense presence is a statement of a commitment to **participation**. It says, "I am not going to collude with a reality that attempts, actively or passively, to exclude, ignore, or suppress those who face profound challenges. I am going to live my life with them. I am not going to think in terms of 'us' and 'them.' I am going to recognize that everyone's life is full of challenges and afflictions, and while those faced by this person may be different in degree, they aren't different in kind. Being with this person may need a different approach to that which I'm accustomed to employing in many of my interactions, but, like needing to learn a language or adapting to a different diet, it may prove as rewarding as—even better than—my other relations." (Participation may be the heart of many interactions with disability, for example in the way people with disabilities seek full access to society and reasonable adjustment to make such access possible; but these are not the concerns of this chapter, which is largely addressing those whose challenges are such that full access is beyond aspiration and where any conventional life-interactions may seem out of reach.)

Presence recognizes that there are sighs too deep for

words. The 1990 film *Awakenings* tells the story of a number of patients in the 1920s who entered a catatonic state through an epidemic and remained in that state until a doctor in the 1960s discovered a new drug that could finally bring them out of that state—although the tragedy of the film is that the drug's effects are not permanent. In an astonishing scene, a patient not only comes round and wakes up, but realizes he has been asleep for forty years, and also perceives that the woman in front of him, whom he dimly perceives as his mother, has remained faithfully with him throughout that almost unimaginable period. The gift that she gave him was the gift of presence, of just showing up until the moment he finally awakened. That woman's witness is close to the heart of incarnational ministry.

Presence and a commitment to participation do not in themselves, however, prevent the paternalism that invariably believes it knows best for a person, or the myriad forms of often well-meant ministry that configure things only in terms of what a person lacks and what I thus assume I am expected to give. Which is why presence must quickly yield to **attention**.

Almost all persons facing one of the four kinds of challenges I listed at the outset know what it's like to feel ignored, discarded—as if others assume or wish they were just not there. And they know better than most (because it happens so rarely) what it means to be truly seen. Attention means focusing all your energies on the gift of the person in front of you. It means laying aside your preoccupations, your own desire to be noticed, putting away your distractions, your texts and instant messages and plans for the rest of the day, setting down your preconceptions, projections, and assumptions, and truly beholding this person in all her uniqueness and difference and complexity and particularity. It means dropping all excuses and disinclination to engage, and being truly with her.

And that requires some verification, some validation, some openness to correction. "I can see you're trying hard to say something." "I see you've left some food on your lap. Have you finished or might it help if I put it back in your hand?" "You look hot. Does it feel good if I put a cold towel on your forehead?" And it behooves one paying attention to be aware of one's own ambivalence about being truly seen. God says to Moses, "I have *observed* the misery of my people who are in Egypt; I have *heard* their cry on account of their taskmasters. Indeed, I *know* their sufferings" (Exod. 3:7). Jesus says to the disciples, "Even the hairs of your head are all numbered [by your heavenly Father]" (Luke 12:7). God pays attention—the one "who keeps Israel will neither slumber nor sleep" (Ps. 121:4). This is no faraway, distant God. This is a God whose attention is wholly rapt upon us. But contrary as we are, having complained that no one notices us, we shrink from such close attention. We bemoan our surveillance culture, and when banks or internet search engines or government agencies pay us constant attention we call it spying. The idea that God gazes at us all the time makes us nervous, caught up as we are in our own anxiety and guilt; and quickly we project onto God an assumption of perpetual judgment and disdain. Even once we accept that God beholds us with loving attention, that God's every wish is to encourage, inspire, restore, and empower us, we willfully hide from God's gaze, saying we're suffocated and worn out with all this constant attention and need some time to ourselves away from the spotlight.

Attention means imagining what it would be like to be truly seen, seen and known, known and understood, understood and forgiven, forgiven and accepted, accepted and enjoyed, enjoyed and celebrated, celebrated and loved, loved and cherished. That's what God's loving attention means. That's why Simone Weil calls true attention "the rarest and purest form of generosity."[1] Rather than giving a person things, like food, clothes, or money, paying true attention means giving a person yourself, your time, eyes, stillness, focus, energy, grace. More than generosity it's perhaps better expressed as true hospitality, because in paying attention to someone you're making space for her to discover, explore, risk, experiment, relax, wonder, articulate, imagine—and take down her guard.

Yet that's where again our resistances kick in. We're nervous of receiving such profound attention, lest in such moments the person giving it perceive our inadequacies, our games, our lies, our blemishes. But we're even more reluctant to bestow on someone our whole attention, because (in Iris Murdoch's word) it's a kind of "unselfing" that leaves us nothing in reserve.[2] And if we do invest in the person the kind of love that attention truly requires, we fear we'll run out of love and become impossibly vulnerable—vulnerable if the person really does have characteristics that make us squirm, and even more vulnerable if we pour all our generosity and hospitality into someone who will one day let us down, or die; or both.

But without attention, without close recognition of particulars, without seeing details and noticing small alterations, without recognizing the reality of what living means for a "challenged" person, life is a fantasy of distraction, false assumption, unchecked projection, and idle superficiality. If we truly want to be with a person, it's no use just tossing material goods or entertainment or gadgets at him. Everything depends on the details: finding what she's truly afraid of, learning why she likes to sit in the dark even on a sunny day, discovering what is the best moment of her waking hours, hearing what skills she can build on. Without atten-

1. Simone Weil, *First and Last Notebooks* (Oxford: Oxford University Press, 1970).

2. Iris Murdoch, *The Sovereignty of Good* (London: Routledge, 1970), 77–104.

tion to such things, trying to help is simply flattering one's self-importance or assuaging one's guilty conscience. God doesn't redeem the world with a lazy sweep of the hand like a millionaire writing off a bad debt. God in Christ redeems creation one creature at a time, with loving attention to redeeming the details of our folly and sin as well as to affirming our goodness and kindness. That's why the cross is so painful—because there God is forgiving us with meticulous attention, one excruciating sin at a time. Attention means offering a challenged human being the rarest and purest form of generosity—one's real, sustained, wholehearted attention—exactly what God gives to us. Does it seem that such attention is hardly going to change the world? Perhaps it's the only thing that ever has.

Mystery and attention, to be received as genuine and not prevaricating, need to be accompanied by **partnership**. A challenged life is one that assumes and requires partnership. That's its unchangeable flaw in some eyes; in the estimation of being with, that's its signature gift. It creates community; its dependence is an invitation to the discovery of the interdependence at the heart of things; it explodes the pervasive but pernicious myth of the independent self-made autonomous human god. Two things are required for partnership with a challenged person. One is that everything the challenged person can do, she is expected to do: satisfaction and reward lie not in how many things are done, how quickly, or even in some cases how well; it lies in the manner in which things are done, with due credit, empowerment, and initiative lying with the challenged person. There is, in the end, no objective scale of value to reward the number of crossword puzzles completed in a lifetime; but for one person, on one day, to answer, or perhaps write the answer to, one single clue may be a pearl of great price. Simply filling in lots of crossword puzzles while the challenged person looks on is not ministry, attention, delight, or partnership;

it's the substitution of a fleeting sense of productivity for the genuine cost and reward of engagement.

The other thing required for partnership is that those who are seeking to be helpful are open to any part of their personality, any one of their gifts, known and hidden, to come to the fore. A straightforward partnership is one where one person is sight-impaired and can't drive, and being with that person may involve driving them to see the doctor or go shopping. But most partnerships are more subtle and more complicated than that. The forces shaping a relationship are almost never wholly, and seldom primarily, those concerning the disability or condition in question: they are invariably as much if not more characterized by the history of the relationship, the respective parties' own previous relationships that have a bearing on this one, and the respective parties' self-understandings outside and beyond this partnership. "But I thought I was taking your time—I thought you'd be bored," says one party. "You have no idea," says the other. "When my husband left me, I thought no one cared if I was alive or dead—and then suddenly you needed me, for things I could actually give you, and I've never craved anything as much as I looked forward to seeing you and you needing me so much."

The 2014 film *Pride* tells the true story of a group of lesbian and gay activists in London in 1984.[3] They realize that the way society, media, and government despise them is equivalent to the way the same forces think about the miners, who are in the midst of their titanic struggle with the Thatcher government. The lesbian and gay activists get it into their heads to reach out to depressed mining villages in South Wales, and, after a series of rejections, they are surprised and delighted to get a reply from the village of Onllwyn. The film shows how, with patience and forgiveness, grace and solidarity, and a lot

3. *Pride*, directed by Matthew Warchus (BBC Films, 2014).

of courage and resilience, prejudices on both sides are gradually broken down and an extraordinary alliance grows up. The film ends with coachloads of miners coming unanticipated to join the 1985 Gay Pride march in London. It's an astonishing turnaround. Together these two groups of stones that the builders have rejected set aside bitterness and self-pity and find they've become one another's cornerstone. A bunch of misfits beautifully, movingly, somehow fit together. These groups aren't challenged in the way this chapter is considering; but they do know social rejection, and their partnership illustrates what partnership can be, while demonstrating that partnership comes best when both parties have a sense of their own neediness and isolation.

The important thing with partnership is that, because it's a form of working with that can always, in the circumstance of profound imbalance of physical or mental challenge, risk lapsing into working for, it never becomes an isolated dimension, and it is always surrounded by attention and delight. Otherwise the gift of the challenged person, and of her apparent limitations, can quickly turn from a mystery to be entered into a problem to be overcome, and the criteria for overcoming that problem may be whittled down to speed, efficiency, and smoothness. In a train the engine and the carriages both have a vital part to play: it's pointless if the engine becomes decoupled from the train, even if the engine gets to the destination sooner; it has ceased to be a train. Likewise a partnership is only a partnership if both parties are playing their part.

The significance of **delight** becomes clearer in the case of what may seem the most distressing kinds of challenge—the baby with multiple disabilities, likely to live only a few weeks or years, and the person with late-stage dementia, apparently absent from all conventional interaction, beyond reach, let alone help. This is the heart of being with the challenged: the situation that seems, outwardly, to be all scarcity with no positive. What positive can be found, and what does being with involve in such cases?

To be with a person in such circumstances is to let go of so much that contemporary culture takes for granted: progress, visible results, cure, tangible reward, success, connection, technologically driven achievement. Being with in these circumstances means leaving aside such impulses and assumptions. In that alone one may find a level of freedom, innocence, ingenuous existence. But it takes a degree of renunciation, patience, and humility, too. Because almost all the things one is accustomed to bringing to a relationship— one's interests, energy, curiosity, questions, stories, intellect, humor—are largely irrelevant. And that means, by having no use for or interest in the attributes with which one is used to presenting oneself—perhaps selling oneself—to the world, the deeply challenged person is already serving by revealing to one so many conventionally hidden parts of one's personality. What it would generally take a skilled counselor or therapist many sessions to uncover, a profoundly challenged person may be able to reveal relatively quickly. If a person is able and willing to make such discoveries, there are countless ones to be had. Who am I when I can't charm or amuse or persuade my dialogue partner? What am I when language has no power? What happens to me when I can't configure every interaction as one designed to achieve an end product? When this other person seems in a prison of oblivion and yet is smiling, why is it that I, this free agent that roams as I please, am the one feeling excluded from the joke, the experience, the realm of reality? What are these other, urgent, pressing events and interactions that I fill my life with, such that I have to withdraw from this person who seems just as easy if I am here or not—are all my urgent interactions attempts to distract me from this unfathomable, apparently purposeless level of existence? Is this interaction confronting me with a level of reality that the rest of my life is a desperate attempt to protect me from? These are among the questions being with the profoundly challenged constantly evokes.

But, in addition to the way challenge turns the tables on the person determined to be helpful, there is also authentic delight. This person expresses the sheer wonder of being alive. For all the attention on what is lacking—look how much is there! A baby with multiple disabilities is yet a phenomenon to behold: how do the coming together of egg and sperm bring about such a creation? What a form of beauty she is—not conventionally made, yet bringing her own quality of amazement and awe. And, while conventional forms of learning, growth, and development may be out of the question, there can be different calibrations of discovery, significant expression in the eyes, a quality of attention or perhaps pleasure. Such moments, rare as they may be, can enrich one's experience by training one to cherish small mercies as deeply as great ones, to see all achievement and reward as relative, to point out the folly in conventional desires and the joy in minute particulars. By being so obviously needy, such a profoundly challenged person can unearth in parents or caregivers love they never previously knew was there, imagination and resourcefulness they never had cause to draw upon, patience and endurance that may make them stronger and more tender people to face obstacles and threats later in life. Such need simply makes one's heart grow—makes one's soul grow, obscuring all in the world that is not love. Each separate insight may seem less than exact delight, but put such insights together and there's a wealth of discovery and truth disclosed in a place many would describe (and all might expect to experience, at times) as a desert of deprivation.

One parent spoke thus of the experience of being with a profoundly challenged daughter who lived just a few years, and never spoke, or walked, or fed herself:

She was really better at entering into the different phases of being with than I ever was or will be. It was she who grasped the mystery of who I was, committed to seeing my abundance and not my deficit. It was she who was able to be so much more present to me when I was always dashing around, she who was the one who was so trained in the art of attention and of seeing me. Some might say that's because of everything else she couldn't do. I prefer to see it as a genuine gift that she was able to give me herself and be a place of true hospitality.

For me, she was, in body and soul, a living sacrifice, in the way that she was there to enable me to discover something of the truth and mystery of myself and of God. She wasn't envious for the life she didn't have and, as the wonder of her being was revealed to us, neither were we. I remember a group of clergy coming to pray for her, the "healers" coming to the "sick"; and being overwhelmed by the realization that if for one moment they had eyes to see, they would know that it was the other way around.

Once you have grieved and let go of the life that should have been, then the wonder of the thin place, which gives such clarity to one's perspective on life, is so incredibly glorious. When you can let go and embrace a challenged child like ours, their lives feel so much simpler than the children who are not challenged in the same way. Thus the profoundly challenged change the way the rest of us live. It's up to us, their companions, to be true to their invitation to be more like them—or at least to live our lives with something of the clarity and perspective they have. I eagerly anticipate resurrection because I think it will feel more like being with the profoundly challenged than not: our glory will be in being more like them.[4]

4. Personal correspondence, January 12, 2016.

This is, needless to say, not everyone's experience. But it aptly conveys what it means to know the delight of being with. **Enjoyment** is a more comprehensive dimension than delight. It encapsulates all the six dimensions that precede it. While delight subverts a narrative that assumes bleakness, deficit, and scarcity, enjoyment counters an instrumentalism that endlessly defers fulfillment, instead insisting that by the power of the Spirit God is fully incarnate here, now, giving us everything we need to encounter, recognize, respond to, and embody Christ's ways. To enjoy one another in the face of extreme physical and mental challenge is to recall that, at the three definitive moments of his time among us, Jesus was profoundly challenged: at his birth he was wrapped (the narrative mentions this detail three times) in swaddling clothes, unable to move freely—not an uncomfortable experience, but nonetheless a constraining one; at his death he was crucified, his hands nailed to right and left, rendering him incapable even of scratching his face, and his legs doubtless similarly disabled; and immediately prior to his resurrection he was wrapped in grave clothes and incarcerated in a tomb, behind a large boulder. At all three defining moments he knew profound, imposed restriction; at one, indescribable pain, and, at another, impenetrable confinement. And yet these were the three key moments in disclosing what it means for God to be with us: at Christmas, the lengths to which God goes, the eternal purpose, and the fragile vulnerability undergone to be with us; on Good Friday, the cost, the agony, the sacrifice, and the relentless commitment of being with us; and on Easter Day, the unstoppability, irrepressibility, and final destiny of being with us. For those seeking to be with the deeply challenged, Christmas demonstrates that being with is the heart of all things, Good Friday manifests that there is nothing we can go through in which Christ cannot accompany us, and Easter Day confirms that the agony and fear and grief will one day be over, and all that will be left will be the joy. To enjoy a person facing profound challenge is to realize that one has entered this threefold experience and revelation; not to deny the distress and sadness, not to downplay the discomfort and sense of injustice, not to take away from the bewilderment and despair—but to realize that, in and through such things, one has been drawn into the mystery of creation and salvation, of God's utter commitment to be with us, now and forever.

And this discloses the paradox of **glory**: that only in letting go of the impulse to make things well—to bring cure, healing, transformation—and only in ceasing to cling on to the life that should have been, the flourishing existence one had every reason to expect, the rational, nimble interactions the rest of the world takes for granted; only in letting these wholly understandable reflexes go, letting them loose, letting them wander away and die, can one begin to see the glory. For the glory lies in resurrection, in a being with that has all the intensity of temporal being with but lacks the dislocation and dismay, retains the characteristics of personality and identity but lacks their damaging and negative features. The more we are bewildered by this life, the more eager we are for resurrection: and in this sense, perhaps in this sense only, in the context of being with the profoundly challenged, it makes sense to speak of glory. And the glimpses of glory in this vale of tears come when resurrection is allowed to break in: and that happens only when we stop clinging to one another that we may hold on to life, and allow ourselves to be with one another knowing that the Holy Spirit, the torn hands of the Son, and the broken heart of the Father will never let us go.

CHAPTER 11

Being with the Dying

Love is strong as death. This is the premise of Song of
Songs. This is the conviction at the heart of Christianity.
This is the context that means being with the dying is the
defining moment of being with.

Why? Because dying is the antithesis of working for.
It's everything working for strives to avoid. The central rationale of being with is that it's the only mode of relating
in the face of impending mortality—when there's nothing
that can be fixed, and all anyone can do is try to face what
lies ahead. We're all dying, of course: dying persons haven't,
in fact, crossed over to another realm of being—they've just
become more acutely conscious of a condition that pervades
all existence. But they've become the embodiment of everything humanity most fears: finality, the unknown, and the
possibility of utter isolation. That doesn't mean there isn't
often a lot of working for to be done: in the last stages of life
a person may need a great deal of practical care, both with
sanitation and with medication, and there are a host of more
practical things that can be done in readying the possessions
and dwelling place for what will follow their departure. As
ever, being with doesn't abolish or remove the need for work-

ing for: it simply provides the purpose of working for and highlights ways a retreat into working for can be a distraction from something more important.

Being with the dying comes in two kinds—two kinds that arguably emerge in all forms of being with, but are most acutely disclosed in the face of mortality. There's being with those who recognize, as best they can, what's in prospect, have taken stock of what can and cannot be done, and are resolved to use aright the time that is left to them on earth; and there are those who are trying as hard as they can not to name or entertain what lies ahead, who whether by distraction or denial are raging against the dying of the light, whose thoughts are squarely on keeping what they know, rather than anticipating what they don't know. The two kinds are not utterly distinct—there's traffic between them. But being with means offering companionship worthy of the courage of the former, while gently but firmly refusing to collude with, and pointing beyond, the despair of the latter.

As often, being with begins with **presence**. The disciples were, for the most part, not with Jesus when he died—the Gospels record that the two Marys and Salome were there, or that Mary and the beloved disciple were there, but that most of Jesus's followers had fled. Was this out of concern for their own safety? Or was it at least partly because they couldn't bear to watch Jesus die? The ministry of presence resembles the practice of the slaves in the parable of the talents who were given five or two talents and took them to market to trade with them. Presence risks clumsiness, the inability to find the right words or to hide squeamish inhibition—it takes one's being "to market" and opens oneself to unknown outcomes. The third slave in the parable, who buries his one talent out of fear of doing or saying the wrong thing, avoids presence—just as it's possible to avoid the first step of being with the dying.

To be with a person in desperate straits when one has nothing practical to offer—no solution, no fix, no precious information, no resolution of the person's predicament—is a vulnerable, exposed place to be. And this is why being with the dying is the definitive form of being with: because in almost every other case there's something—however small—that one can imagine offering a person in distress; but in this case there really is nothing—and yet that awareness of one's empty hands is the beginning of ministry. When it's clear there's absolutely nothing one can do, one faces a profound parting of the ways: a powerful impulse urges one to go elsewhere, to find another setting, a context where there is something one can do, a place where one can again imagine a world where one's skills and gifts and wisdom can make things better, turn things around, achieve results, and create energy—an alluring theater of escape. Death is the ultimate dose of cold water thrown over such magic dust. In such circumstances, presence, perhaps better called abiding, is a pledge to the person dying that one's own need to be useful and effective is of lesser significance than the person's need for company, understanding, and solidarity. It's also a statement of faith that being with represents a truer reality than working for, both within human existence and within the heart of God.

In this sense dying persons and those who are with them experience a deeper dimension of living than those who are not dying—or who, at least, are not so conscious of the unavoidable imminence of death. The great majority of human endeavor and activity is revealed to be precisely what it is—ancillary to the truest form of existence, which is being with one another. Those who are dying present their actual and potential companions with the moment of truth: Can you be with me when there's no hiding in the realms of working for me? If you say, "I can't be with the dying, I have to attend to the living," are you not really saying, "I can only cope with being around those who are not yet aware or willing to name that they are dying"? Presence with the dying is thus a statement, to oneself and to others—not just to the dying persons themselves—that we are all dying, and that there's nothing more important than time spent with those who are entering the last stage of life.

The practice of **attention** is about recognizing that every death is different: every person approaching the end has her own particular concerns and fears, doubts and convictions, regrets and expectations. The traditional preparation for death—the confession of and absolution from sin, the handing over of one's life into the hands of God, trusting in the atoning death of Christ—focuses, almost inevitably, on the aspects one can name, address, and thus to some degree control: events of the past that can be described, repented of, and forgiven, elements of the Christian faith that can be articulated, identified with, and responded to. But the very nature of death is precisely a convergence of everything we can't control. The plaintive question, "What will become of me?" has no straightforward answer. The best answer is, perhaps, "God created all things to be with you and redeemed all things to restore that relationship: I trust that God will be with you even more tangibly beyond death than now, and my desire to embody that is the reason I'm sitting here with you at this very moment." But the practice of attention is more about listening to the many layers of the question than about hastening to answer it. The busy offering of readings and prayers and counsel and visits and reassurance may be largely a reluctance to stay in a place of silence and powerlessness and the unknown. If a dying person doesn't articulate the question, "What will become of me?" it may be less because she doesn't want to know or doesn't want to seem frightened than out of fear of exposing the fragility of her companions and provoking a superficial or manifestly inadequate answer.

Being with is both about abiding in the ordinary moments and about not flinching in the somber and perhaps terrifying moments. There's a place for graveyard humor: death and its proximity turn conventional expectations upside down and relativize so much of the self-importance of habits the world takes for granted: such is the stuff of irony and satire and wry humor. Besides, close attention discloses that few people can sustain a level of intensity for very long. Being with means being prepared and willing to talk about news and events, reflections and frustrations one moment, and flip to fears and wonderings, panic and despair the next. A diagnosis that death is impending may initially seem to change everything: but not everything changes, both because ordinary things like cooking meals and engaging with other people's lives carry on, but also because everyone is dying, and proximity to death is more about a difference of degree than of kind. Paying attention is the way companions show that they are prepared to let this death impact them as existentially as it affects the person going through it. It means entering a level of existence in which one single fact takes precedence over all others. But it also means letting the dying person's perception of that fact shape and color one's own engagement and response. There is no objective estimation of what's taking place: there's only the dying person's narrative, and such complementary or counternarratives offered by those around them. Attention regards the dying person so closely that her perception of her own narrative becomes clear and, allowing for any confusion brought on by a condition or course of treatment, takes appropriate precedence.

Of course there's an overwhelming sense of deficit—of a life that might have been longer and perhaps more fulfilling, relationships that could have endured to the next rite of passage, friendships that never had the chance to flower, projects that will never come to fruition, dreams never to be fulfilled. But **mystery** names the dimension of being with that discloses a truth beyond that immediate shock and wound of deficit—truer living, firmer hope, deeper joy. Rather than see the dying person as drowning in a whirlpool, and companions stretching out their arms from the water's edge to hold on to those arms as tight as they can for as long as they can, mystery turns things round and sees them from the other end: it is the dying person who has insight, wisdom, perspective, and discernment, and the companions want to stay close to the dying person, not to offer distraction and good cheer, but to receive the gold that only the dying person can give. That's what it means to be with people in the spirit of the parable of the last judgment: to see Christ's face in the face of the dying person is to expect them to speak words of revelation, of truth, and, paradoxically, of life.

This is not about maudlin parting words or pious attempts to crystallize life's essence in a pithy epigram. It's about staying still in the place of transition from time to eternity, from now to forever, from the ephemeral to the everlasting. This is holy ground, where the mystery of death reflects back on the mystery of birth, where length of days pales into the shadows before realities beyond depth or measurement or conception. Dying persons are isolated from the fervid world of news headlines and economic swings and urgent emotions and the flotsam of opinion and judgment: but they are correspondingly more in touch with the heart of existence, the wonder of fragile breath, the inexplicability of consciousness, the lightness of being. Mystery refers to the way being with a dying person highlights the breadth of such quality in life when the quantity of life seems thin.

It's perhaps impossible truly to enter into the depth of mystery without first acknowledging, articulating, and perhaps in some sense performing a depth of lament. Lament identifies the paradox of this terror, this horror, this final ending, set against and in the context of God's overflowing, relentless, never-ending love. The juxtaposition of the two makes the former intolerable and incomprehensible, the reality of the latter makes it possible to speak of the former without utter despair; but only after a truthful rendering of the bewilderment and terror of the former can any exploration of mystery begin with integrity. The howl of pain, fear, anger, and isolation must invariably precede any discovery of a reality beyond that bleakness.

It may seem absurd, even thoughtless, to speak of **delight**. But delight is the appropriate name for the cherishing that constitutes the rites of the last hours. It is a beautiful thing to take a person's hand, and recall with gratitude the countless things this hand has touched and held—perhaps the large hand of the person's own mother, the tiny hand of an infant, the texture of a working implement, the bread of holy communion—and anticipate what it will come to hold: the water of the river of life. It is a tender thing to touch the ear of a dying person and remember with dignity the myriad of sounds that ear has heard—words of love, sounds of the dawn chorus, cries for help, songs of hope—and imagine what it will come to hear: the word of God. It is a profound thing to meet a person's eyes, and name with thanksgiving the panoply of sights those eyes have beheld—the fire of a sunset, the birth of a child, the kindness of a stranger, the spectacle of a great work of art—and await what they will still gaze upon: the glory of the Trinity. It is a rare thing to touch a person's nose, and speculate with gladness on those smells that nose has known—the fresh-baked dinner, the rose in summer, the perfume of exotic allure, the incense of holiness—and realize what it will perhaps soon inhale: the joy of God's desiring. It is a privilege to come close to a person's lips, and reflect with awe on what the person's tongue has tasted—the soft fruit, the daily bread, the refreshing drink, the wine of the Lord's table—and perceive what it will duly taste: the cup of the kingdom.

All this is delight. Delight sees what is there, not what isn't there. Delight describes a way to be with dying persons that rejoices in their life, both in itself and as a token of all life. There may not be many smiles; there may be no laughter; there may be tears and numbness and dismay; but this cherishing of what has been given, and this trust in what it indicates of how much more is yet to come, is a practice of delight that indicates how all life may be cherished, at all times.

Perhaps the most poignant dimension of being with the dying arises in relation to **participation**. Participation is the epitome of with—the discovery that it doesn't matter what we do, provided we do it together. And dying we do not do together. Even if we were to do it at the same time, we do not do it together. David goes up to the chamber over the gate, and cries, "O my son Absalom, my son, my son Absalom! Would I had died instead of you, O Absalom, my son, my son!" (2 Sam. 18:33): but he can die neither with nor for Absalom. Absalom dies alone. Everyone does. Being with can take the horse to the water of death; but it cannot drink that water together. This is the isolation, the loneliness, the separation that constitutes, for many, the most painful aspect of the whole experience. Living is more than anything about being with God and one another: dying is done alone. Awareness of this casts a shadow but invites humility at every stage of the journey. For may be a pointless, though understandable, distraction; but at the very last, even with has its limits.

Where participation fails, all the more may **partnership** arise, somewhat in its stead. With partnership the recognition that there are some things best left to the respective partners (rather than always done together) always risks lapsing into working for. But provided partnership comes in the context of mystery—the awareness that dying persons have in some ways a privileged and more accurate perspective than anyone trying to "help" them—the most acute of these dangers can be averted. The principle "never do for someone what they can perfectly well do for themselves" continues to apply—in many respects normal life goes on, and to turn a person's last months or weeks into a continual party in which they are indulged with treats and attended upon like medieval royalty is simply another avoidance—a further instance of the impulse to turn being with into working for.

Partnership may be as simple as a companion doing the grocery run for a dying person yet seeking to involve her as much as possible in preparing the meal itself. It may be a joint effort in which the dying person explores any revisions to her will while a companion records those alterations, secures signatures, and involves lawyers. Perhaps more tellingly, it could involve a companion asking the question, "Do you think there's anyone with whom you feel a reconciliation is necessary and possible, or for whom a legacy gift might be significant and treasured, with whom I might help you to get in touch or whose whereabouts I might seek out?" In this form, partnership is a kind of working with that assists a dying person to be in the company of those that might be harder to be with. The real work, for example of reconciliation, is something the dying person can only do for herself: but the facilitative work, of asking the question, perhaps discovering if a conversation on both sides might be welcome, is an act of partnership, a form of working with. Again it requires a change of heart that sees proximity to death as not just a time of loss and calamity, but as a unique opportunity to have long-overdue conversations and offer often-inhibited or overlooked gestures of gratitude or kindness.

But the key dimension of partnership doesn't lie in useful actions and kind interventions. It lies in making a virtue of the tragic limitations of participation. It breaks one's heart that a companion cannot ultimately accompany the dying person at her moment of direst need. Participation meets its match. But precisely because the companion is not immediately facing the abyss of oblivion that many fear lies beyond our last breath—precisely because the companion is on the riverbank while the dying person goes under the waves—the dying person may find she can say certain things and express degrees of feeling that, were the two in exactly the same predicament, would be impossible to share. Just as a child can pummel a parent's chest with the frustrations of life, not yet realizing that the parent shares such inner despair but has found a way to live with it; and just as a person in trouble speaks with a counselor and puts into words her deepest fears and regrets and hurts, under the understanding that both parties will set aside the fact that the counselor, too, knows such pain and loss and anxiety; so being with the dying can mean, for companions practicing this dimension of participation, a willingness to draw a veil over their own bewilderment so that the dying person can let it all spill out, go to the very bottom of the pond, trust that there is nothing that can't be faced, and thus find strength to endure the unendurable. Partnership can involve the wordless and understated sharing of tasks and activities; it can mean provoking one another into acts of courage and hope; but most importantly it means saying, "Just at the moment I'm stronger than you are, in physique or resilience or faith: lean on me while you do the things you so desperately need to do."

The more political dimensions of being with become apparent when we turn to **enjoyment**. Enjoyment means relishing the life of the dying person, rather than judging that life as useless for advancing some ulterior good or as intolerable in the light of its degree of pain or hopelessness. The

logic of the consumer economy and of commodified interactions is to regard the human body as a tool or instrument
for garnering experience, sensation, and gratification. If it's
not working to achieve those ends, it must be disposable.
The fact that it can't be replaced by anything else doesn't always seem to break the logic. The point is that the body is a
mechanism, something you use to acquire or accumulate or
mediate something of greater value. To identify this isn't to
uphold the opposite mistake—that the body is a final good,
whose embellishment and beautification is the object of life.
Instead, the characteristic of enjoying the embodied nature
of dying persons is to cherish them as a fragile but unique
enfleshed reality, to be treated as a priceless gift for so long
as their life can be lived without egregious technological
intervention.

To suggest that such a life should be intentionally ended,
for example by euthanasia or assisted dying, is to assume
something that contradicts the practice of enjoyment. It regards physical pain or emotional isolation as so unendurable that the only compassionate response is to hasten the
patient's death. But this presupposes that, when working for
has failed, the contribution of being with is negligible. Enjoyment has no reason to question that working for often—
indeed, ultimately, always—fails. But that is all the more
reason to practice the dimensions of being with, and to appreciate their value. It is as if the failure of working for, in
the face of extreme pain, is intolerable—and so working for
must be reasserted, this time in the form of mercy killing.
But what is required is not a revised working for: what's required is being with—an enjoyment that not only affirms
a companionship that endures the most unspeakable distress, but continues to find delight and mystery amid even
the most unfathomable hardship.

The experience of extreme pain constitutes the most

troubling circumstance of being with the dying, one that calls, as enjoyment does, upon every previous dimension of being with. It requires presence, a presence that says, "I am not going to be frightened away by having to watch you in agony and despair." It needs attention, an attention that says, "I can see the veins on your forehead, the red flecks in your eyes, the horror of what this is costing you." It necessitates mystery, mystery that says, "You are entering a realm of suffering few ever know, and there is no answer to why you are being expected to go there." It involves delight, delight that says, "I am continually amazed how you continue to give blessings to me and to those around you even in the midst of this excruciating distress." It entails participation, even to the extent of saying, "I will be with you as long as it takes, but I realize the worst of this you have to face alone." And it calls for partnership, for all that can be done to alleviate the pain must be done. Enjoyment provides no magic dust, no panacea; it's not naïve about how miserable such existence can be. But it represents the best that humanity can be—patient witness in the face of terrible suffering.

It may seem absurd to speak of **glory**. Sometimes dying persons attain a level of peace and acceptance that radiates and blesses those around them. It could be that the willingness of those with dying persons to embody the dimension of delight enables them to articulate wisdom, grace, and insight that promise to remain in the memory of their companions for a long time. It may also be that, like the martyr Stephen, dying persons see the heavens opened and Christ standing at the right hand of the Father. The most heartening reward for being with dying persons is to witness the dignity, courage, and faith that they may embody. Not always, of course— medication, injury, pain, fear, doubt, or denial may make such experiences rare and precious, but not uncommon.

Glory is perhaps more often discerned in retrospect than

as a conscious, lived experience. A more sober, yet tender realization may emerge from reflecting on the dimensions of being with dying persons. It concerns the nature and essence of life. Since earthly existence isn't permanent; since it isn't without disappointment, distress, and despair; since such wisdom and faith as are to be had come at least as much in adversity as in comfort; and since intimacy, trust, companionship, and love are as much to be desired as any gift, the parties close to the dying person may discover that what they have shared is as significant as anything they have ever known. If being with is the purpose of incarnation, creation, and salvation; if that purpose is most fully practiced in being with one another; and if being with one another finds its apogee in being with the dying, then one may rightly conclude that such an experience, for the companion at least as much as for the dying person herself, constitutes the defining experience of one's life. If heaven is to offer more tenderness, more solidarity, more passion, and more transparency than this, heaven really must be pretty special. This is what it means to speak of glory.

Precious, Honored, and Loved

Not long ago I was doing a live broadcast on the radio. Just before I came on, the producer brought in the man who was next on after me. Now, speaking live to about 5 million people can be quite sobering, but this man was about as nervous as anyone I've ever seen. His hands were shaking so much he could hardly keep hold of the piece of paper on which he'd typed out the things he really didn't want to forget. The creases on the slip of paper indicated how much he'd fretted over it the night before. But on it were five short lines.

And that struck me. If you were about to face the scariest conversation of your life, and the night before you were too nervous to write an aide-memoire so you typed five short lines, I wonder what they'd say. Israel in Babylon was facing the scariest time of its life. And on a piece of parchment, or some kind of a scroll, the prophet Isaiah recorded the five things Israel needed to remember (Isa. 43:1-7). In the fashion of a number of scriptural passages, they're written in a chiastic structure—that's to say the first line is echoed by the last

A sermon preached at St. Martin-in-the-Fields, London, England, on January 10, 2016.

line, the second line by the penultimate line, the third line
by the third line from the end, and so on—so the fifth line,
the one right in the middle, is the one that really counts. It
becomes like the point of an arrow. I want to look at the five
things Isaiah tells us, because I've got a hunch they're not just
speaking to exiles in the sixth century BC: they're speaking
to you and me, right here, right now.

The first thing is, God created you. That's created, not
manufactured. Everything manufactured is a product. Everything created is a miracle. Your creation in the womb is
like the creation of the world: it's a thing of limitless wonder,
complexity, care—a mixture of biology and poetry, a blend of
the physical and the spiritual—and it happens not randomly,
but for a reason. God made you because God wanted you,
and had a job that only you could do. And it says God formed
you. So creation wasn't a once-for-all thing: God continues
to craft you, like a potter with clay on the wheel, deftly and
painstakingly, with wisdom and skill and attention.

Then the second line on the scrap of paper is, God has set
you free. This part really goes into the depths of our soul. It
says, "Do not fear." Everywhere in the Bible people encounter God and they're terrified. They're terrified by God's holiness—but also by their own shortcomings. "Do not fear"
means God sees you, God knows you, God understands you,
God forgives you. You don't have to have any secrets from
God. You don't have to play your usual games. God's beyond
all that, and sees you beyond all that. God has redeemed you.
I don't know if you've had the experience of being in a restaurant and you get a bit greedy and the food all costs more than
you meant it to and you start the edgy process of asking for
the bill and wondering how you'll divide it up; and then your
companion comes back from the restroom and you find he
has already paid. Paid the lot. You feel embarrassed and grateful and relieved all at the same time. God has redeemed you.

You've been set free; the wrong you've done is forgiven, the damage you've done God is putting right, the hurt you've inflicted God is healing.

But your fear isn't just that your wrongdoing will catch you out. Your deeper fear is that your life is meaningless, that you have no ultimate significance and belong nowhere. God says, "I have called you by name, you are mine." You know how they say a mother can recognize her baby's cry even in a crowded room? That's how God knows you. God made everyone, but regards you as if you were the only one. God has called you by name. When someone remembers your name, you know either that person is very special, or you're very special to that person. God knows your name. Your real name—not the one everyone else calls you. Your real and intimate name. And you belong to God. You may feel you've spent your whole life not fitting in—wrong face, wrong time, wrong manners, wrong accent, wrong looks, wrong everything. Now you belong. And belonging in God, you are everywhere at home. Some people say, "There's always a place for you at my table, always a place on my sofa, always a bed if you're thrown out." That's what God says. But with God, it's forever. You are mine.

And the third line on Isaiah's parchment is, "I am with you." Now notice what this says and what it doesn't say. It doesn't say bad things won't happen. You'll be deluged by seas. You'll be flooded by rivers. You'll be beset by fire. Tragedy, disaster, conflict, and defeat will happen. There's no promise here that you'll live a charmed life and nothing will worry your pretty little head. But see what it does say: you'll be deluged by seas, but you'll pass through them, and I'll be with you. You'll be flooded by rivers, but they'll not overwhelm you, and I'll be with you. You'll be beset by fire and flame, but it won't burn you up or consume you, and I'll be with you. You'll face pain, terror, loss, grief, shame, horror, calamity, but I'll be with you. I'll hold your hand. I'll walk with you. I'll be there. I'll never leave you alone. Some while ago I had a very painful surgery and when I came round I was hyperventilating and was convulsed with tears, and the friend who'd accompanied me to the hospital just gave me the most enormous hug. He said nothing, but just enveloped me in sweater and shoulder and everlasting arms. That hug said, "You've done a hard thing. But I'm here." It still hurt. But that hug said, "You're not alone. I'm with you." I haven't forgotten that hug. I never will. God says, "I am with you."

The fourth line on the scrap of paper is more mysterious. It seems to be about God exchanging one people for another. But you don't have to have a scholarly knowledge of ancient Near Eastern archaeology to get what it's saying. God says, "I'll make sacrifices for you. To be with you I'll give up some other important and valuable things. I could be elsewhere, in richer places, more comfortable surroundings, softer touches, easier rides. I know you: to be with you isn't going to be a rose garden. But I'm going to do it anyway." And in the New Testament that language of "I'll give up everything for you" takes on a whole new dimension. In Jesus, God really does give up everything for us.

And that brings us to the fifth line on the parchment. There's a reason why Isaiah doesn't start here. It's partly a historical reason: what we've read so far more or less works its way through the Old Testament and through the story of Israel: the creation to start with, then the liberation from Egypt, then the covenant on Sinai in which God says, "I'll be with you," and then the cost of God choosing Israel when Israel is what they call in the northeast of England a "worky ticket," like a niggly soccer player goading the referee to send him off. But it's partly also a psychological reason: God says, "I made you, I saved you, I'm with you, I gave up everything for you." And it begs the question, Why? It's a question that comes out of gratitude, because what God's articulating is grace, totally unearned, unwarranted, undeserved relationship and blessing. It's also a question that comes out of skepticism—why, knowing what I'm like, would anyone say such things to me? What's the catch? What's the let-down at the end of all this glory? So the fifth line is the answer to this suspicious yet grateful, mystified yet humble, question: Why am I all these things to you?

And this is God's answer. You can really do this answer justice only if you imagine both parties in tears: you in tears because you've been trembling with fear and doubt since your first conscious breath, a fear that there was no meaning and a doubt that, if there was, you'd be included in it; and God in tears because it takes so many ways and so many times to persuade you and encourage you and show you. Here are the words that are the center of scripture, the essence of Christianity, the heart of it all: "Because," says God to you, "you are precious in my sight, and honored, and I love you."

The first two words complement each other. "You are precious" means "You are of infinite value, you are unique, you are without compare." "You are honored" means "I respect you, you have your own integrity, there's more to you than simply your relationship with me." And then, the final word: "And I love you." You need all three words. I don't know if anyone's ever told you they love you when it was clear they didn't honor you. It's actually not very nice at all. And to be loved and honored is great, but without the "precious" it makes you feel the person's just being kind. Precious, honored, loved: you need all three.

And this is where what I earlier called the chiastic structure of Isaiah's words really works. Because we're all familiar with the phrase "God loves you" and how shallow and superficial it can sound. But it's not shallow here, because it's the climax of these five layers of glory; and then those five layers cascade back down in more or less reverse order once we've reached the top of the mountain. This, we see, is where love comes from—and this, we go on to see, is what love entails. To say "I love you" means something only if it's the last piece in the jigsaw—backed up by actions and faithfulness and promises kept and commitment proved.

So here are the five memory phrases about God, according to Isaiah. I crafted you; I set you free; I'm with you; I gave up everything for you; I love you—so, in reverse order, I gave up everything for you, I'm with you, I saved you, I formed you.

Imagine the shape of this poem as an arrow, with the fifth phrase, "You are precious, honored, and loved," as the point of the arrow. And where is that arrow pointing? It's pointing right at Jesus. At Jesus's baptism the voice from heaven says almost the very same words—"You are my Son, the Beloved; with you I am well pleased." Precious, honored, and loved. And at Jesus's baptism there are the voice and waters and Spirit of creation, the parted river of liberation, the solidarity of Jesus being with us, and these precious and honored words of love. Jesus's baptism is the performance by God the Holy Trinity of the prophecy of Isaiah 43.

Remember those five declarations that God made to Isaiah, that the voice said to Jesus, and that the Spirit whispers to you. Write them or type them onto paper and seal them on the inside of your soul. Remember them in the scariest moment of your life. They're the heart of it all. You are precious, honored, and loved: now, and forever.

Index of Names and Subjects

Acts, book of, as a journey from Jerusalem to Rome, 85
Adam Bede (Eliot), failed pastoral conversation in, 133–38
Addiction, 28, 53, 157; as an analogy for sin, 53
Alford, Henry, 72
Ananias and Sapphira, 95
Anxiety, 1–2, 5; as the root of most of the deadly sins, 2–3
Apology, 152
Aristotle, on virtue, 55
Attention, 12; and being with the afflicted, 169–70; and being with the called, 120–26; and being with the challenged, 190–93; and being with child, 107–8; and being with the creation, 64–66; and being with the dying, 204–5, 212; and being with God in prayer, 27–29; and being with God together, 82–85; and being with one-self, 54–55, 58; God's attention, 191; and peace, 158; and reading poetry, 30–31
Atwater, Ann, 166
Augustine, 13, 41, 74
Awakenings (1990), 190

Bailey, Kenneth, 45n3
Baptism, 20, 38, 57, 82, 92, 111, 114–15, 117, 122; as communion, 38; and participation, 115; and partnership, 115
Barth, Karl, on prayer, 38
Being afflicted, 21, 146, 147, 185
Being called, 21
Being challenged, 21, 146, 185; kinds of challenges, 185
Being a child, 102–3
Being for, 10
Being gentle, 56–57
Being grateful, 55–56
Being humble. See Humility
Being hurt, 21, 146, 147
Being one's own size, 56

Being a person of praise and
blessing, 57
Being troubled, 21, 147
Being with, 7–13, 20–23; the
central rationale of, 201;
and rejection of the problem-solution axis, 9. See
also Attention; Delight;
Enjoyment; Glory; Mystery;
Participation; Partnership;
Presence
Being with the afflicted, 168–
84 passim; and attention,
169–70; and delight, 172–73;
and enjoyment, 179; and
glory, 179; and mystery, 168,
170–72; and participation,
173–75; and partnership,
175–78; and the prayer of
transfiguration, 178–84; and
presence, 168–69
Being with the called, 114–32
passim; and attention,
120–26; and delight, 127–28;
and discipleship, 116; and enjoyment, 128–30; and glory,
130–32; and mystery, 126–28;
and participation, 114–15;
and partnership, 115–17,
127–28; and presence, 117–20,
120–21. See also Discern-
ment; Elijah and Elisha, and
taking up the mantle; Holy
Spirit: and calling
Being with the challenged,
185–200 passim; and attention, 190–93; and delight,
195–99; and enjoyment,
199–200; and glory, 200; and

mystery, 186–88; and participation, 189–90; and partnership, 193–95; and presence,
188–90
Being with child, 20–21, 99–113
passim; and attention, 107–8;
and breastfeeding, 105–6;
and church relationships,
110; and conception, 102,
105; and delight, 108–10;
and enjoyment, 111; a
father's ministry, 101; and
glory, 106–7, 113; as Mary's
ministry, 113; a mother's
ministry, 101; and mystery,
101–3, 107, 113; parenting as
working for, 106; parenting
as working with, 106; and
participation, 104–5; and
partnership, 105–6, 109; the
phrase "with child," 104;
pregnancy as a template
for, 112; and presence, 110;
and procreation, 101; what it
means to be a child, 100–101;
what it means to be a parent, 100–101, 110; the word
"child," 102; as working for,
106; as working with, 106–7.
See also Marriage; Pregnancy
Being with the creation, 63–79
passim; and attention, 64–66;
and delight, 66–69; as discipleship, 63; and enjoyment,
76–78; as fundamentally
about worship of the cre-
ator, 63; and glory, 78–79; and
humanity as part of the creation, 70; and mystery, 66;

and participation, 69–71; and partnership, 71–76; and pet dogs, 76–77; and presence, 63–64; as worship, 63
Being with the dying, 21, 201–13 passim; and attention, 204–5, 212; as the definitive form of being with, 201, 203; and delight, 207–8, 212; and enjoyment, 210–12; and glory, 212–13; and mystery, 206–7, 209, 212; and participation, 208, 212; and partnership, 208–10, 212; and presence (abiding), 202–4, 212; two kinds of, 202; and working for, 201–2
Being with God in prayer, 24–42 passim, 81; and attention, 27–29; and delight, 35–37; and enjoyment, 40–41; and glory, 41–42; and the Holy Spirit, 26; and lament, 29–30; and mystery, 29–35, 87; the offertory prayer of the Eucharist, 36–37; and participation, 37–38; and partnership, 24–27, 38–40; the prayer of commission, 92; the prayer of discernment, 92; prayer as a dismantling of isolation, 25–26; prayer as the first event of the day, 25, 27–28; the prayer of incarnation, 40, 179; the prayer of intercession, 38–40, 85, 92, 96, 178; the prayer of lament, 29–30; prayer as nonverbal communication, 24; the prayer

of participation, 37, 38; the prayer of resurrection, 40, 179; the prayer of thanksgiving, 36–37; the prayer of transfiguration, 40, 178–80; and presence, 24–27; and thanksgiving, 36
Being with God together, 20, 80–98 passim; and attention, 82–85; and collective decision-making, 95–96; and delight, 88–90; and enjoyment, 96–98; and gatherings for other purposes, 82; and gatherings to pray, 81–82; and glory, 98; and mystery, 85–88; and participation, 90–92; and partnership, 92–96; and presence, 80–82. See also Baptism; Being with God in prayer; Eucharist, the
Being with the hurt. See Peace
Being with oneself, 43–62 passim; and attention, 54–55, 58; and delight, 58; and enjoyment, 60–61; and glory, 61–62; and the inevitability of death, 53; and mystery, 55–58; and one's basic survival, 50; and one's flourishing, 50; and one's well-being, 50; and participation, 58–60; and partnership, 60; and presence, 51–53; when life is distressing, 51–52; when life is dull, 52–53
Being with the troubled, 143–45; asking "Is that the

whole story?," 144; enabling one's story within the scriptural story, 143; inviting one to explore further and explain more fully, 144; staying with the formless and void until one can find words and weave together silences, 143–44. See also Adam Bede (Eliot), failed pastoral conversation in; Burial Rites (Kent), pastoral conversation in Berwick-upon-Tweed, and Russia, 147–48

Bible, the: as a love song, 34; as a parable, 33–34; as a poem, 31–32; as a prayer, 34–35; reading of, 30; as the story of the peace process carried out between God and human beings, 164; writing of and the Holy Spirit, 34

Blake, William, 56

Blame, 171

Blasphemy, 41

Body, the, commodification of, 211

Bourbon dynasty, 151

Bruce, Robert, 64–65

Burial Rites (Kent), pastoral conversation in, 138–45; and attention, 141; and enjoyment, 142–43; and glory, 143; openness to mystery and delight, 141–42; and participation, 142; and partnership, 142; and presence, 141

Cain and Abel, 159

Calling. See Being with the called

Calvin, John, 54

Catechesis. See Education, Christian

Causae et Curae (Hildegard of Bingen), 54

Caussade, Jean de, 53–54

"Centuries of Meditations" (Traherne), 42, 68–69, 78

Chaplaincy, 118–19

Chisholm, Thomas, 65

Church, the: as the body of Christ, 163; definition of, 81; and Greek ecclesia, 80. See also Being with God together

Climate change. See Ecological crisis, the

"Come, Ye Thankful People, Come" (Alford), 72

Communion, 37–38; baptism and the Eucharist as forms of, 38; and Greek koinōnia, 37; and Latin communio, 37

Confession, 152–53; in corporate worship, 84–85; two moments of, 26–27

Confirmation, 82, 117

Consumerism, 25

Conversion, 111, 155

Cotter, Jim, 45

Crafting Prayers for Public Worship: The Art of Intercession (Wells), 39n3

Creation, the. See Being with the creation

Creator-creature distinction, 85–86
Cullinan, Tom, 50n4
Culture and the Death of God (Eagleton), 162

David: and the death of Absalom, 208; as a shepherd boy, 63–64
Dear White Christians: For Those Still Longing for Racial Reconciliation (Harvey), 154–55
Death/Dying, 21, 53, 146; dying as the antithesis of working for, 201; the typical preparation for death, 204. *See also* Being with the dying
Deferral, 2, 5
Delight, 12; and being with the afflicted, 172–73; and being with the called, 127–28; and being with the challenged, 195–99; and being with child, 108–10; and being with the creation, 66–69; and being with the dying, 207–8, 212; and being with God in prayer, 35–37; and being with God together, 88–90; and being with oneself, 58; and peace, 153
Del Vasto, Lanza, 50
DePaola, Tomie, 174–75
DePrince, Michaela Mabinty, 180–82
Dimensions of being with. *See* Attention; Delight; Enjoyment; Glory; Mystery; Participation; Partnership; Presence
Disabilities, and participation, 59–60, 189–90
Discernment, 92, 95, 114, 115, 119, 121, 123
Disciples (the Twelve): and Pentecost, 123, 124; in the upper room, 122–23
Discipleship, 14, 115–16; and being with the called, 116; being with the creation as discipleship, 63; and the home, 119; and one's close relationships, 14; overlapping of with ministry, 14–15, 99–100; overlapping of with mission, 18–19; as prior to, and foundational for, ministry and mission, 116–17; as relationship with God, with one's self, with other Christians, 14
Doctrine, false, 160
Dumm, Thomas, 44

Eagleton, Terry, 162
Ecological crisis, the, 71, 72–75; and the global poor, 73–74; and God, 74–75; and governments and corporations, 72–73
Education, Christian, 90–91; and calling, 119
Elijah and Elisha, and taking up the mantle, 123–26
Eliot, George, 133–38
"Elixir, The" (Herbert), 65–66
Ellis, C. P., 166

Enjoyment, 13, 41; and being with the afflicted, 179; and being with the called, 128–30; and being with the challenged, 199–200; and being with child, 111; and being with the creation, 76–78; and being with the dying, 210–12; and being with God in prayer, 40–41; and being with God together, 96–98; and being with oneself, 60–61; and peace, 157; and prayer, 40–41; as a teleological practice, 129–30

Enlightenment, the, and the self, 43

Envy, 2, 5, 187–88

Eternal life, 79, 92

Ethics, 165–66

Eucharist, the, 38, 74–75, 81–82; as a church in microcosm, 82; as communion, 38; and the Holy Spirit, 26; and the offertory prayer, 36–37; and the presentation of the gifts, 130

Euthanasia, 211

Evangelism, 164–65

Evans, Tom, 51–52

Evil, 160. See also Sin

"Faith Matters: Desired Things" (Wells), 58n12

Foch, Ferdinand, 151

Forgiveness, 153, 164; and healing, 146, 171–72

"For the Beauty of the Earth" (Pierpoint), 77

Gandolfo, Elizabeth O'Donnell, 100n1

Global warming. See Ecological crisis, the

Glory, 13; and being with the afflicted, 179; and being with the called, 130–32; and being with the challenged, 200; and being with child, 106–7, 113; and being with the creation, 78–79; and being with the dying, 212–13; and being with God in prayer, 41–42; and being with God together, 98; and being with oneself, 61–62; epitome of (God being with us in Christ), 13; in a human context, 98; and peace, 154

God: attention of, 191; as a character in the parable of the rich fool, 47–49; glory of, 131; the God who is for us, 10; the God who is with us, 10–11; grace of, 187–88; jealousy of, 187–88; in the Old Testament, 10–11

God's Companions: Reimagining Christian Ethics (Wells), 22, 22n3

"God's Grandeur" (Hopkins), 65

God's Hotel: A Doctor, a Hospital, and a Pilgrimage to the Heart of Medicine (Sweet), 54n9

Gospels, the, as a journey from Galilee to Jerusalem, 85

"Great Is Thy Faithfulness" (Chisholm), 65

Greed, 2, 5

Ham, Pete, 51–52
Hamlet (Shakespeare), 70
Harvey, Jennifer, 154–55
Healing, 93, 146, 153; and forgiving, 171–72
Herbert, George, 65–66
Heresy, 160
Hildegard of Bingen, 54
Hippocratic Oath, 56
Holy Spirit, 57, 120; and calling, 126, 127; constant presence of, 25; and the Eucharist, 26; and prayer, 26; and presence, 26; at the transfiguration of Jesus, 183; and the writing of the Bible, 34. *See also* Spiritual gifts
Hopkins, Gerard Manley, 65
Hosea, book of, 30–33; as a parable, 33; as a poem, 31–33
Humility, 35, 55, 57–58

"I Can't Live If Living Is without You" (Ham and Evans), 51–52
Idolatry, 41, 155
Improvisation: The Drama of Christian Ethics (Wells), 22, 22n1
Incarnational Mission: Being with the World (Wells), 14, 22
Industrial revolution, the, 70
Irenaeus of Lyons, 62
Isaiah, memory phrases about God, 214–19
"I Wandered Lonely as a Cloud" (Wordsworth), 67

Jealousy, 187–88; as a teleological sentiment, 188
Jenson, Robert, 70
Jesus, 6, 13, 62; baptism of, 219; in Bethlehem, 122; birth of, 105; as both human and divine, 162; crucifixion of, 42, 57, 162, 163, 193; in Egypt, 11, 122–23; in Galilee, 11, 121; incarnation of, 57, 163; in Jerusalem, 11, 121–22; and Mary and Martha, 3–6; the mystery of his death, 30; in Nazareth, 11, 121; as our peace, 148; as the Prince of Peace, 158; profound challenges faced by, 199–200; resurrection of, 57; transfiguration of, 180, 182, 183; as working with and for, 11. *See also* Parables of Jesus
Jesus through Middle Eastern Eyes: Cultural Studies in the Gospels (Bailey), 45n3
Journey, as a metaphor for life in general or the life of faith, 85
Justice, 160–61
Justification, 38

Kent, Hannah, 138–45
Kocher, Abigail, 39n3

Lament, 29, 207; and sin, 29–30; and suffering, 29
Laying-on of hands, 94
"Lines Composed a Few Miles above Tintern Abbey, On Revisiting the Banks of the

Wye during a Tour, July 13, 1798" (Wordsworth), 67–68
Living without Enemies: Being Present in the Midst of Violence (Wells and Owen), 7, 7n1, 8, 10, 14
Loneliness, 44–45
Loneliness as a Way of Life (Dumm), 44

Marriage, 101–2; as a long-term exercise in being with, 102
Marvell, Andrew, 86
Mary (mother of Jesus), 47–48; and the conception of Jesus, 105; her ministry of being with child, 113
Mary and Martha, 3–6, 49; Martha's criticism of Mary and Jesus, 4–5; Martha's service, 6; Mary and presence, 24; Mary's service, 6; and transgressing against social norms, 3–4
Maslow, Abraham, on the hierarchy of needs, 50
Mead, Margaret, 159
Mindfulness, 61
Mindfulness: A Practical Guide to Finding Peace in a Frantic World (Williams and Penman), 61n14
Ministry, 7, 14–20, 115–16; and the church building, 119; incarnational ministry, 19–20; ministry of the self, 92–96; ministry of skills, 92–96; ministry of the Spirit, 92–96; ordained ministry,

15–17; overlapping of with discipleship, 14–15, 99–100; overlapping of with mission, 19
Mission, 18–19, 63, 97–98, 115–16, 166; incarnational mission, 19; overlapping of with discipleship, 18–19; overlapping of with ministry, 19; and the place of work or study, 119
Mission trips, 118
Modernity, and the self, 43, 44
Mothering as a Metaphor for Ministry (Percy), 100n1
Mountbatten, Lord, on Gandhi, 55–56
Murdoch, Iris, on "unselfing," 192
Mystery, 12; and being with the afflicted, 168, 170–72; and being with the called, 126–28; and being with the challenged, 186–88; and being with child, 101–3, 107, 113; and being with the creation, 66; and being with the dying, 206–7, 209, 212; and being with God in prayer, 29–35, 87; and being with God together, 85–88; and being with oneself, 55–58; and the death of Jesus, 30; as the opposite of a problem, 12, 29, 195; and peace, 148–51; and sin, 29–30

Nazareth Manifesto, A: Being with

God (Wells), 7, 7n1, 8, 10, 11, 13, 14, 22
New creation, 78–79
New Jerusalem, 78
New Testament, and salvation, 47
Niebuhr, Reinhold, 52
Now One Foot, Now the Other (dePaola), 174–75

"Ode: Intimations of Immortality from Recollections of Early Childhood" (Wordsworth), 101
Old Testament: and security, 47; as a study in perceiving the God who is for us and the God who is with us, 10–11
Owen, Marcia A., 7, 7n1

Parable, 33–34; discovering one's life as a parable, 34
Parables of Jesus: the parable of the late-hired laborers, 187; the parable of the rich fool, 45–49; the parable of the talents, 98, 131, 202
Participation, 12–13, 37–38; and baptism, 115; and being with the afflicted, 173–75; and being with the called, 114–15; and being with the challenged, 189–90; and being with child, 104–5; and being with the creation, 69–71; and being with the dying, 208, 212; and being with God in prayer, 37–38; and being

with God together, 90–92; and being with oneself, 58–60; as communion, 37; difference of from partnership, 37; and disabilities, 59–60, 189; and Greek *koinōnia*, 37; and interactions with disability, 189; and Latin *communio*, 37; and peace, 160. *See also* Baptism; Eucharist, the
Partnership, 13; and baptism, 115; and being with the afflicted, 175–78; and being with the called, 115–17, 127–28; and being with the challenged, 193–95; and being with child, 105–6, 109; and being with the creation, 71–76; and being with the dying, 208–10, 212; and being with God in prayer, 24–27, 38–40; and being with God together, 92–96; and being with oneself, 60; difference of from participation, 37; and peace, 151
Paul, transfiguration of, 183
Peace, 147–67 *passim*; as an aspiration, 148, 150; and attention, 158; and delight, 153; as dynamic, 149; and enjoyment, 157; and glory, 154; Jesus as our peace, 148; and mystery, 148–51; and participation, 160; and partnership, 151; the peace process, 150–54, 161; and presence,

Index of Names and Subjects

161; and the Trinity, 148–51.
See also Violence
Penance, 152, 155
Penman, Danny, 61n14
Pentecost, 123, 124
Percy, Emma, 100n1
Pierpoint, Folliott Sandford, 77
Poetry, reading of, 30–31
Postmodernism, and the self, 43–44
Power and Vulnerability of Love, The: A Theological Anthropology (Gandolfo), 100n1
Prayer. *See* Being with God in prayer
Prayer at Night: A Book for the Darkness (Cotter), 45
"Praying Animal, The" (Jenson), 70
Preaching, 93, 94
Pregnancy, 104–5; and agency, 104; as "being with child," 104; as a template for being with child, 112
Presence, 11–12; and being with the afflicted, 168–69; and being with the called, 117–21; and being with the challenged, 188–90; and being with child, 110; and being with the creation, 63–64; and being with the dying, 202–4, 212; and being with God together, 80–82; and being with oneself, 51–53; and peace, 161; and prayer, 24–27
Pride, 2
Pride (2014), 194–95, 194n3

Problem, 12; as the opposite of mystery, 12, 29, 195
Prophecy, 93–94

Quest, medieval notion of, 85

Reconciliation, 153, 155, 165, 177; and a dying person, 209; and the role of an intermediary, 177–78
Repentance, 52, 152, 155
Resurrection, 153–54, 162, 200; of Jesus, 57
Roberts, Charles, 155
Roberts, Marie, 155

Sacrament of the Present Moment, The (Caussade), 53–54
Sacraments. *See* Baptism; Eucharist, the
Salvation, 42, 150, 153–54, 165, 166; as a peace process, 153
Sanctification, 38
Saying "sorry," 154
Self, the: the Enlightenment's assertion of the self, 43; modernity's quest to establish the self, 43, 44; and the parable of the rich fool, 45–49; postmodernity's self as a chimera, 43–44; as the soul in scriptural terms, 45. *See also* Being with oneself
Self-loathing, 52
Shakespeare, William, 64, 70
Shaping the Prayers of the People: The Art of Intercession (Wells and Kocher), 39n3
Simon the Pharisee, 4

Sin, 29, 53, 159–60; addiction as an analogy for, 53; the difference between sin and evil, 160; and lament, 29–30; original sin, 86
Sloth, 2
Social media, 2, 53
Song of Songs, on love as strong as death, 201
Sonnet 94 (Shakespeare), 64
Sontag, Susan, on illness, 170
Spiritual gifts, 93–94. See also Healing; Preaching; Prophecy
Stephen, 212
Stewardship, 94–95
Suffering, 29; and lament, 29–30
Suicide, 52; assisted suicide, 211
Sweet, Victoria, 54n9

Thanksgiving, 36
Tithing, 95
"To His Coy Mistress" (Marvell), 86
Traherne, Thomas, 42, 68–69, 78
Triangulation, 4
Trinity, the, 13, 150; dynamism of, 149; nature of, 42; and peace, 148–51. See also Attention; Delight; Enjoyment; Glory; Mystery; Participation; Partnership; Presence

Vegetarianism, 75–76
Veil, metaphor of, 180; and the afflicted, 183–84; and apathy, 181; and deprivation, 181; and

isolation, 182; and Moses and the Israelites, 182–83; and prejudice, 181–82; removed by the Holy Spirit at the transfiguration of Jesus, 183
Violence, 148, 155–62, 164–65, 166–67; by Christians, 159–61; collective violence, 157; as fantasy, 155–57, 164, 166; as idolatry, 155; as insurgency, 157; as oblivion, 156–57, 164, 166; personal attack, 157; and the rule of law, 158; state-sanctioned violence, 157; why Christianity has not healed the virus of violence, 159; why there is so much violence when Jesus is the Prince of Peace, 158–59
Vocation. See Being with the called

Weil, Simone, on true attention, 191–92
"We Plow the Fields, and Scatter" (Campbell), 71
Wesley, Charles, 30
Wesley, John, 61
Westminster Shorter Catechism, Q. 1, 40, 40n4
What Would You Do? (Yoder), 161
Wilde, Oscar, 60–61
Williams, Mark, 61n14
Wilson, Leonard, 103
Wordsworth, William, 66–68, 101
Working for, 8–9, 13, 49, 93; and

concentration of power in the expert and the highly skilled, 8; as the established model of social engagement, 8; parenting as, 106; and the problem-solution axis, 8–9

Working with, 9, 13; and concentration of power in coalitions of interest, 9; and the problem-solution axis, 9

Worship, 62, 74–75, 77; being with the creation as worship, 63

Yoder, John Howard, 161

Index of Scripture References

OLD TESTAMENT		130:1-2	51	18:20	81
		139:7	26	18:21-22	164
Genesis		139:13-14	105	19:14	100
1:27	70			20:1-15	187
1:28	70	Ecclesiastes		25:24	117
3	27	3:1-7	60	25:36	83
4	27			26:52	157
28:17	87	Isaiah		28:20	81
		9:6	158		
Exodus		43:1-7	214-19	Mark	
3:7	191	64:1	11	1:13	71
				2:14	120
2 Samuel		Hosea		3:35	100
18:33	208	1	31-33, 34	8:34-36	50-51
1 Kings		NEW TESTAMENT		Luke	
17:6	71			7:9	120
19:9	120	Matthew		10:38	3
		1:18	105	10:40	4
2 Kings		13:8	120	10:41-42	5
2:1-14	123-24	16:26	117	12:7	191
		17:2	180	12:13	49
Psalms		18:2-5	100	12:16-21	45-49
121:4	191	18:3-4	60	18:11-12	39

Index of Scripture References

19:10	83	Romans		1 Thessalonians	
22:19	81	13	84	5:16–18	35

John		**2 Corinthians**		**Revelation**	
1:5	164	12:2–4	42	21:1–2	78
1:14	13			21:3	78
10:10	186	**Ephesians**		21:5	78
11:4	179	2:14	148	21:23	78
17	42	2:14–16	163	22:1–2	78
				22:20	81